KHJ, LOS ANGELES: BOSS RADIO FOREVER

WOODY GOULART

DEDICATION

I dedicate this book to **Samuel C. Glass, Jr.**

I have never loved or felt closer
to any other person in my entire life.

I am so grateful to him for
decades of support and encouragement
that he has given me
for my storytelling and my art.

FOREWORD

By Evan Haning

For convenience, we'll call it "youth culture," and it crashed over us, wave after wave: beatniks, rock and roll, folk, protest music, the British invasion, hippies, political protest, recreational drug use, the psychedelic sound, pop art, acid rock, heavy metal, disco. These waves were disorienting, their intensity unrelenting. But as we young swimmers bobbed and tried to keep our heads above water, others were surfing the waves. Masterfully riding each swell, they seemed perfectly at ease, in this tsunami of change.

These Silver Surfers, disc jockeys, were members of a profession that has disappeared, for all practical purposes, and it is very difficult to even describe its appeal to anyone who grew up without them.

But let's try.

As Woody describes in this book, it is hard to imagine a world where music was not instantly available on demand. The first place most of us heard a new song was on the radio, and the only way to get a copy of it was to buy it at a record store. There was no YouTube, no Pandora.

It was also possible, if you had access to a tape recorder, to put the mike next to a radio and let it roll. If you were lucky, the song you wanted might be played. But even if it was, the quality would be bad, and the first ten seconds would be marred by a jingle and a disc jockey chattering about the time and temperature.

Remember, it wasn't until recently that copies of all kinds were hard to obtain. You used carbon paper to keep copies of high school book reports. To get copies of a photograph for family and friends, the developer at the drug store would need the negative.

So copies of all kinds were hard to duplicate, whether texts, images or sounds. Originals had more value then, before the digital revolution made most content easily reproducible.

As Woody well describes here, hearing new songs was not one lazy click away, as it is now. The main source for new music was radio, specifically the stations teenagers listened to. Because they were few in number, they had enormous power over which records were heard and bought. And their audiences were loyal.

Top disc jockeys in major cities enjoyed a celebrity comparable to that of rock stars. When I went to work at KRLA in 1973, the awe was tailing out (sadly for me!), but the stories I heard were amazing.

KRLA was a 50,000-watt powerhouse (and competitor of Drake-Chenault's blockbuster KHJ, of which you'll soon learn more in Woody's account) located on the grounds of Pasadena's Huntington-Sheraton Hotel.

The staff told me that as many as 300 teenagers would crowd the lobby and parking lot—sometimes as late as midnight—hoping to see the jocks or visiting musicians.

Disc jockeys were often encouraged to show up for work during the last record played by their predecessor, and to leave during their last record, to avoid being mobbed by the kids.

Super groups such as The Beach Boys would arrive at KRLA and KHJ in a limousine to hand-deliver their latest single. Same as the kids, the jocks were important them.

Woody worked with two of the most influential radio personalities in the neon fun jungle that is Los Angeles, Robert W. Morgan and the Real Don Steele. These two men were arguably the best Top 40 disc jockeys ever on the air, anywhere.

There were other "greats and near-greats," of course: Wolfman Jack, Dave Hull "the Hullaballooer," Johnny Hayes, Charlie Tuna, the "Master Blaster," Bill Balance, Gary Owens, and more in Los Angeles.

San Francisco, New York and other cities were home to other legends: Johnny Holliday, Dr. Don Rose, Cousin Brucie, Don Imus, Murray the K, Dick Biondi and Jimmy O'Neal, among them.

But this book is a personal memoir whose heart and soul is deeply connected to the adventurous rock and roll radio programming created, perfected and executed nearly 50 years ago by Bill Drake and Gene Chenault, and Woody is very well positioned to tell that story.

He and I started in radio more or less at the same time, in San Luis Obispo, California, where Woody grew up. We worked at KVEC, a small but locally important station that provided morning and afternoon news blocks, local college sports, and music. The format was called MOR for middle-of-the-road or "Chicken rock," which mixed softer Top 40 hits with adult standards. Think Tony Bennett and the Bee Gees.

Like most young disc jockeys, we loved what we were doing, but didn't want to do it too long in this particular town. Our mail was delivered locally, but our heads, hearts and futures were in Los Angeles.

I got there before Woody, landing a spot on KRLA, a station I loved, which had long been around. KRLA, the Big 11-10 had been home to "Emperor Bob" Hudson, Dave Hull, Bob Eubanks, Johnny Hayes, Casey Kasem (later host of *American Top 40*), and a satirical news team called The Credibility Gap, that was a precursor to *Saturday Night Live*). It featured Harry Shearer, David L. Lander, Lew Irwin and others.

But by the time I arrived, KRLA was practically vacant. Johnny Hayes and I were on tape, the only two voices on the station, heard around the clock. We aired one 30-second Sears commercial per day at around 4:50 p.m., Monday through Friday.

Such was my first professional engagement in the neon fun jungle.

Although I found work in Los Angeles first, Woody was lucky enough to land among Top 40 radio's performing and programming royalty. He was also lucky enough to have the observational intelligence and wit to understand the importance of what he saw, to appreciate and preserve it.

The broadcast world Woody writes about no longer exists, of course. Howard Stern has no need to race from his studio to a waiting car. There are no teenagers crowding the parking lot outside XM/Sirius.

In fact, disc jockeys, as such no longer exist. There are radio personalities and talk show hosts, but apparently there is no longer any business need for cultural gatekeepers—Boss Jocks, Good Guys, what Bill Drake described as "hip older brothers" to introduce new songs, generate excitement, bestow "validation" on teenagers, and do whatever else they did.

The job description may be gone, but many of the jocks that were intelligent and flexible enough to adapt are still broadcasting. Don Imus and Robert W. Morgan became talk show hosts. The multi-talented Johnny Holliday is the play-by-play voice of University of Maryland basketball and football, and a sportscaster on national network radio and television.

Enjoy Woody's story. And if you are occasionally puzzled by his enthusiasm, try to use your imagination. Think of what it would be like if the music you wanted to hear was only available on two or three places on a radio dial.

Imagine a high school classroom with a magazine photo of the Beatles taped to the door. A teacher's handwritten message at the top of the picture warns, "Haircuts for failure? See Below!"

On some school mornings you see a vice-principal with a ruler measuring a boy's hair to see if it touches his collar. If it does, his parents will be called to take him home until he's had a haircut.

And on Friday afternoon you and your buddies pile into a friends' car, turn on the radio, which warms up in a few seconds, and crank it up to hear …

"It's THREE O'CLOCK in Boss Angeles, with ME! The REAL DON STEELE on a FRACTIOUS FRIDAY! It's a GOLDEN WEEKEND, baby … an we're (unintelligible) as we head out on our QUEST for ADVENTURE into the NEON FUN JUNGLE! (garbled) … MERCY, baby!

And The Beatles sing:

There's nothing you can know that isn't known.
Nothing you can see that isn't shown.
Nowhere you can be this isn't where you're meant to be.
It's easy.

Evan Haning
Washington, DC
November 2011

INTRODUCTION

We Americans typically create huge signs in public places to share with others what we believe is important to us. In New York City, just take a look at Times Square and you'll see with your own eyes what I mean. In Las Vegas, even people with short attention spans will know from the brilliantly bright neon lights and the screaming video screens what's considered important. We are not a subtle culture.

I believe that radio broadcasting in the United States of America existed primarily for the transmission of culture. That seemed to be its core purpose for many decades. Half a century ago this core purpose for radio was clearer than ever before or since. In the mid-1960s on the fabled Sunset Strip in Hollywood, California there stood a splashy, self-congratulatory sign in a very public place that was erected for local gods of rock and roll radio. They were deemed to be important to the culture of that era. The gigantic billboard had no neon and no video. It was all just text and faces. You can see a photograph of the billboard online at www.bossradioforever.com. But, the faces were significant because they belonged to several young men who had become culturally significant merely because they all worked at one Los Angeles radio station. That station was Boss Radio KHJ. Today, the billboard is gone and the radio station is gone.

I will forever remember one of those young men from the Sunset Strip billboard. He was known as The Real Don Steele. He irreverently and sarcastically referred to Los Angeles as the **neon fun jungle**. It was a cool phrase that even 50 years later remains one of the most accurate and unforgettable nicknames that LA has ever been given.

You will still find a lot of neon there. You may or may not find fun, depending on how you define that for yourself. But, without a doubt, Los Angeles remains a jungle where day-to-day survival can be challenging and risky.

I was fortunate to have worked with The Real Don Steele at another Hollywood rock and roll radio station in another decade. He was a product of Hollywood, itself. He had been born there and even graduated from the famous Hollywood High School. Although he lived only 61 years, his was a unique and memorable life like few others have known.

Steele invited his radio listeners on "*a quest for adventure in the neon fun jungle*." For him, that phrase conveyed his urgent message to us all: Seek excitement. In the search, you never know what you may find. I found that attitude especially captivating and motivating.

I wrote this book especially for people who were not yet born in 1965. Why should anyone want to remember Boss Radio KHJ or think about the neon fun jungle? The simple answer is this: I believe that we are inseparable from our culture. If we expect to know ourselves well, we must learn all we can about our culture.

Previous versions of this book available online were abbreviated and incomplete. So, I decided in 2017 to create the definitive edition you are reading now.

I believe that my work to help you know about Boss Radio KHJ is very unusual. Nobody else ever took the unified approach to communicate with the major players and preserve their memories and opinions like I did. What you're reading now is a deliberately different kind of rock and roll radio history. Simply put, it was not written from merely one person's perspective and I weave everything in one story. Here you will find multiple perspectives from different people all brought together in one place told as a story. This book is your gateway to travel back in time to a culture very unlike what we've got in the United States today.

Bob Dylan best described the era when he observed how the times were a-changin'. The transition from the 1960s into the 1970s proved to be extraordinarily turbulent. Unusually vivid and sometimes explosive cultural and political twists and turns in American history were common in those days. The rules also were very different back then compared to today. You may find it difficult to believe that such an unpredictable time ever could have happened in our country.

But, this is nonfiction. This stuff really did happen. Some of what happened certainly will seem just a little bit strange compared to today. Or maybe not. Today has become strange in a different and very special way of strange, even when compared to the 1960s.

Some of us still have our mental faculties today even though we survived the 1960s. Perhaps we lived so that we could tell what we experienced. That time was known as the psychedelic era. It was as much a state of mind and a way of life that in retrospect differs greatly from any other decade before or since. At the time, you could find very thin neckties, thick-framed glasses, sticky hairstyles that were held skyward against the forces of gravity by aerosol sprays, and an immortal and bold sports car from the Ford Motor Company cleverly named after a very fast horse. It also was a time of innocence and innovation in rock and roll radio.

More importantly, it was a show business environment that no longer exists and likely never will exist again. This is true if only because much of what today's radio broadcasting industry accepts as everyday reality literally was prohibited by federal law back then.

What you're reading now started in the 1990s on a website that I wrote and produced. I maintained the online presence for my history of Boss Radio KHJ for nearly 20 years until somebody hacked my website and did some truly messy damage. The cost in time and money to repair that malicious destruction of content motivated me to switch instead to this version, which is less susceptible to intruders who want to cause trouble.

I have no hidden agendas here. I mean: I'm not selling anything with this book except for fun, insight, and awareness.

Many of the original participants in what became a 1960s-radio programming phenomenon in Hollywood are dead. I have felt a deep sense of responsibility to the original participants to report what happened as accurately as I possible could. And yes, I have encountered disagreement from some of them about what I wrote. I can look myself in the mirror, however, and know that I reported accurately what happened so many decades ago. There will come a day when all who were there in Hollywood on the team of original participants at Boss Radio KHJ are dead. Such is the nature of mortality. I hope that what I have written will help you remember them all and their accomplishments in rock and roll radio back then. For those of you were alive in those days and believe you know what "really happened," I hope you will give due consideration to my reporting and my storytelling here.

If you are just starting out in your professional career, I sincerely believe that you can make your own future if you choose to do so. Don't believe anybody who tells you otherwise. Don't let anyone take away your ability to dream and create your own future. But, you also should be realistic about what careers are likely to continue into the future within radio and television broadcasting.

Everyone can amplify their experience in reading this book by visiting www.bossradioforever.com where there are many rare audio files and photographs from back in the day.

Thank you so much for your interest in my work.

Woody Goulart
Las Vegas, Nevada
May 2017

CHAPTERS

Chapter 1:
Fantasizing about Los Angeles

In May 1965 when one Los Angeles radio station called Boss Radio KHJ redefined rock and roll radio, I was not yet 15 years of age. I lived 200 miles north in the small town of San Luis Obispo, where I found that life was never as glamorous or exciting as it imagined it would be if only I lived in the neon fun jungle.

My hometown is known by its initials, S-L-O. Yes, that certainly branded it as a slow town. Some people even choose to use the nickname of SLO-town. As far as city nicknames go, that certainly will never be as cool-sounding as Motown.

I was unsatisfied with the quality of my life in San Luis Obispo. Even at age 15, I was not interested in living a slow and relaxed life. I longer for a much faster pace of life for myself that I knew was only attainable if I moved to Los Angeles.

The location of San Luis Obispo compared to the location of Los Angeles creates a very real separation between the two places. Nobody could listen to Boss Radio KHJ in San Luis Obispo in the 1960s because the station's signal was not capable of traveling 200 miles north from Los Angeles.

In those days, the dominant radio stations used AM (amplitude modulation) frequencies—one part of the radio spectrum that is still in use today. Nowadays, however, AM stations are where you will most likely find spoken word programming such as talk shows, all-news, and all-sports, or, programming that is presented in a language other than English. AM radio signals are limited by our planet's terrain, weather conditions, and other physical factors beyond the control of us mere mortals.

Boss Radio KHJ was assigned to the AM frequency of 930 kilocycles. In San Luis Obispo there was a local radio station that was assigned to 920 kilocycles. Most radio receivers were incapable of tuning into signals broadcast on adjacent frequencies, so in those days, your best choice was to tune in to AM stations that happened to be broadcasting near you.

How we learned about popular culture was more difficult back then compared to today. We had no internet, no iTunes, or other such wonders that today we take completely for granted. You may wonder how did anyone survive culturally in those days without personal, digital copies (or cloud copies) of music to carry around in a small hand-held device. Well, it was difficult, and I certainly felt that living in SLO-town was the equivalent of isolation far from what I imagined was the magic of Los Angeles media.

A media phenomenon crystalized my motivation to move from San Luis Obispo to Los Angeles. I was only five years old when the ABC Television network started broadcasting an exciting new series named *Disneyland*. Millions of American kids like me were utterly defensively against the persuasive powers of Walt Disney and the magic kingdom that he created in Southern California. The very first visit that my parents took me on to Disney's now-famous theme park and resort in Anaheim redirected my life. As I sat in the back seat of my parents' station wagon, gazing out the windows with wide eyes, I vowed that when I grew up, I would live and work in Los Angeles.

The Importance of Being Mac

But, first I had to grow up. That meant that I had to accept San Luis Obispo radio because it was "the only game in town." The most influential local radio programming during my youth was a country music show hosted by "Mac the Scotch Hillbilly." In reality, Mac was an engaging radio personality whose real name was Don Macleod. He was the first "radio celebrity" I became aware of. I imagined as I listened to Mac that it would be exciting and fun to grow up and be on the radio like him.

More importantly, I learned four lessons from Mac that still are meaningful today:

1—If your career path brings you to on-air work, you do not need to have what's considered a major-market professional radio voice. Mac did not. He was downright down-to-earth and ordinary in how he sounded. Yet, he also was hugely successful if judged by how much money he generated in advertising sales revenues.

2—You need to be real in how you come across on the air. Mac did this so well. He spoke on the air as if he happened to be talking solely to you. This is an essential trait that I think is absolutely missing in much of what I hear on the air today. I have one best example of being real. Wait for it. It's The Real Don Steele. He was so real that he had the word in his brand name!

3—You need to have a brand name. Mac was the first radio celebrity I encountered in my life who had a brand name. Most on-air people have no brand names today. When you listen to such bland and brandless voices on the air, they all blend together like the ingredients thrown together haphazardly into a bad enchilada.

4—As the great American philosopher comic Julius Henry ("Groucho") Marx said: *The secret to life is honesty and fair dealing. If you can fake that, you've got it made.* To some people, this may seem like mere sarcasm. However, to me, this way of thinking embodies the heart and soul of how to have a successful career no matter what profession you may choose for yourself.

I also developed a love of "cowboy songs" as a result of many years listening to Mac on the air. To this day I find it difficult to accept that anyone has written or performed better "cowboy songs" than Hank Williams, Sr. (1923 - 1953). From repeated exposure in those formative years of childhood, I became mesmerized by Mac's choice of a theme song for his highly successful "Ranch House Jamboree" show—Spade Cooley's rendition of Steel Guitar Rag.

Learn by Doing

Seeking to learn what I needed to get into a financially-successful career in radio, I entered the journalism program at Cal Poly State University in San Luis Obispo. Cal Poly was licensed to use one of the few FM (frequency modulation) available on the Central California coast. The call letters KCPR, which stood for Cal Poly Radio, were not too well known locally because the station operated with only 10 watts of effective radiated power and was on the air far fewer than 24 hours a day.

I quickly became news director and eventually station manager at KCPR after working on the air in several shifts as well as doing audio production. KCPR afford me exactly that kind of career preparation that I had been looking for. The station turned out to be a major career turning point in my young life.

One Cal Poly journalism professor in particular, Ed J. Zuchelli, contributed in significant ways to my transition into work in the commercial broadcasting profession. Zuke was always there at the precise moments when I needed either to be speeded up or slowed down in my work and studies at Cal Poly. He also provided me with passionate encouragement to go beyond an undergraduate degree.

Part of our Cal Poly "learn by doing" education involved listening to unedited recordings known within the industry as air checks from Los Angeles radio stations. That is how I first got to hear Boss Radio KHJ.

I experienced culture shock the very first time that I heard recordings of The Real Don Steele. Not kidding. What a jolt it was for me to hear such a rapid-fire delivery from a radio personality who mixed clever word choices with a dry sense of humor! I had grown accustomed to the slow pace in SLO-town of "Mac the Scotch Hillbilly" so, in contrast, listening to Steele was joyously stunning to me.

My fellow college radio pals and I would fantasize that someday we would get to work in what Boss Radio KHJ nicknamed Boss Angeles. We felt a strong lure to move to the neon fun jungle so that we could live and play within a far more exciting social and cultural environment compared to SLO-town. Most of us had visited Los Angeles many times by our late teens and early 20s since the drive took only four hours from San Luis Obispo and in those days a gallon of gas cost only around 30 cents! Although living in LA-LA-Land certainly may have been exaggerated and satirized by television shows like The Beverly Hillbillies—swimming pools, movie stars—the City of Angels was an intense magnet nonetheless for small-town boys and other dreamers, then as now.

College radio instilled in me and my colleagues a motivation to become "good enough" to earn a career working in Los Angeles radio. But, few of us could do much more than merely dream it would happen since making it to Los Angeles radio seemed completely beyond our reach. We felt stuck in small market radio, but we might as well have been living on a distant planet far from Earth.

We did not really grasp the radio technology—why FM stations can travel to distant places while AM stations do not—but we were aware that we could not listen to Boss Radio KHJ over the air while we were in San Luis Obispo. Late at night, however, would could tune in another famous Los Angeles AM station, KRLA at 1110 kilocycles. Somehow, their signal could bounce through the night skies all the way up to us in SLO-town. KRLA at that time with its format of current hit songs and trendy announcers sounded unlike anything we knew from listening to small market radio. KRLA was a breath of fresh air to us.

Listening to tape recordings and late-night signals was how we familiarized ourselves with Los Angeles radio. Of course, we could also get our hands on Claude Hall's essential radio industry column in *Billboard* magazine. His column was how we became aware of rock and roll radio programmers like Bill Drake (1937 - 2008) and Ron Jacobs (1937 - 2016). We hero-worshipped radio celebrities Robert W. Morgan (1937 - 1998) and The Real Don Steel (1936 - 1997), whom we viewed as being worth emulating. I cannot express how grateful I am to have known and interacted with these men in person.

I had a gut-level feeling that none of us in college radio at Cal Poly would actually end up working in Los Angeles radio. We did not have the deep voices or the cool, trendy deliveries that each of the Boss Jocks did. But, since college radio gave us a chance to develop our skills and talents, who could predict what the future might hold. We had a specific format to follow that taught us discipline and precision that we lacked. College radio in that era was largely free-form radio—particularly on noncommercial college stations. But at Cal Poly, we wanted to be different from all other college stations. We wanted to be professional to prepare ourselves to work in the professional world after Cal Poly.

From personal experience, I know how young people in their college years tend to measure the value of their life experiences in terms of freedom—how much you can get away with. If you learn how to mature emotionally as you age, however, you may learn how shortsighted is the preference for freedom to do whatever you want on the air on a radio station. Without careful guidance from professionals who have worked in the real world of broadcasting, a college radio experience can become little more than a few years of escape and play for people who may never even intend to pursue professional careers in radio. That's fine if you're young and you just want the fun of putting unprofessional stuff on the air without the structures and rigors or a format. But, then all that essentially adds up to is an unwise misuse of time, taxpayers' money, and university-owned facilities.

If you're smart and worth anything professionally in communications, you should be able to sharpen your skills and talents while attending college, get your undergraduate degree, and then move up to a professional career in a top twenty media market. That would be solid proof of your skills and talents. Even if you don't remain in the broadcasting field, ending up with a professional career in a top twenty media market will speak volumes about what you've got to give to the world. Choosing to stay working in smaller markets below the two twenty line is fine if that's really what you want for yourself. Yet, there always will be much more for you to accomplish in larger markets, not to mention potentially higher compensation for you.

When I was in college radio, I emerged within a small group of people who wanted to emulate real-world, commercial successful strategies and techniques for how a radio station should sound. We believed that we should shoot for having presentational styles like the major market radio stations. We incorporated professional standards of excellence into our very hearts and souls.

I wonder whether college radio enthusiasts today are being given a proper real-world context and an appropriate audience adaptation mindset to prepare them for major media market careers after they graduate. Apparently, however, the Cal Poly Journalism Department and the "learn by doing" approach there paid off professionally for some of us. Without warning, one of my college radio colleagues from Cal Poly escaped the confines of SLO-town and landed directly in the legendary neon fun jungle. In turn, he opened the doors for me to get hired to work at a Hollywood FM radio station when I was only 22 years old.

Chapter 2:
The Name Game

What I did not realize in my younger days was that there is great wisdom contained in that 1964 *Billboard* top-of-the-charts hit by Shirley Ellis, *The Name Game*. The irresistible song is simple and silly like a child's rhyme, but repeated listening peels away revealing a deeper significance: Giving a memorable name to someone or something often can be crucial to public awareness, acceptance, and acquiescence. Today, we call that **branding**.

This is especially apparent in how radio stations are named and the resulting reputation, identity, and branding that follows. If you happen to be outside of the radio broadcasting business, you probably would never think twice about the name or call letters that a station has been given. But, the call letters can be a core element of any radio station's success or failure.

Call letters have a strange and somewhat twisted history. Radio stations have an older naming convention compared to television stations because the medium of radio was launched first. Go to www.museum.tv/eotv/callsigns.htm if you want to learn more about the history of call letters in United States broadcasting.

11

International agreements were signed about what particular letter would start radio call letters. Canadian radio call letters start with the letter "C" and you may think that was because of the country name. Well, maybe not. In the United States, radio station call letters could start with either the letter "W" or "K" and go ahead, try to figure out the sense in that! I remember that when I was a child, I learned that "K" originally stood for kilocycles (and eventually kilohertz), but that memory could have come from someone who was a trickster.

The most twisted part of the naming game came from how the FCC assigned radio call letters based on the geographic location of the station. If you grew up west of the Mississippi River like I did, you came to know radio stations that start with the letter "K" as compared to east of the Mississippi where the letter "W" is first in the call letters. But, okay, so then what happened in Pittsburgh, Pennsylvania? Why were the call letters KDKA assigned to a radio station in Pittsburgh, which at last observation was located well east of the Mississippi? Maybe because Pittsburgh has three rivers, that whole river-as-boundary thing just befuddled the folks at the FCC so that they ended up saying, "Oh, what the hell, let Pittsburgh keep the 'K'!"

The Dubious Value of Some Federal Regulations

I never had much admiration for the FCC. This is because I happen to believe that taxpayer money should stop being spent on a federal agency that manages frequency usage, judges the content that is broadcast over those frequencies, and what not. The way the FCC responded to a Janet Jackson and Justin Timberlake performance on live network television during halftime at the 2004 Super Bowl was the last straw for me. Paying federal bureaucrats within the FCC using taxpayer money to tell us what is moral versus what is immoral seems to be just plain wasteful to me. Other people who are not funded by taxpayers will be more objective in making such determinations because they aren't accepting money from the federal government. Or, perhaps adults in the United State of America may one day learn to make determinations for themselves of what is moral versus what is not and stop relinquishing that to authority figures of our bloated bureaucracy.

Federal spending should, in my twisted view, go to truly worthy regulations that may have life or death consequences upon the lives of ordinary citizens such as keeping violent extremists from hurting and killing our people within our borders. The FCC is nowhere near life or death in terms of consequences. I believe that the FCC should be privatized—funded and operated by a consortium of media industries representing all broadcasting interests in the Western Hemisphere. That new way of doing business for the FCC should be limited to managing an orderly use of the available frequencies. The regulation of broadcasting industry content should be ended completely once and for all. I urge this because over the decades, attempts to legislate human morality in the United States have been wildly unsuccessful. Google the Eighteenth Amendment of the United States Constitution to see the best example of what I mean.

But, let's get back to the fascinating world of call letters. The reality is that the naming convention for broadcasting call letters prior to the late 1920s differed substantially from what we know today. You need to just accept that KDKA, Pittsburgh was named back in the good old days before the west-of-the-Mississippi versus east-of-the-Mississippi scheme. No surprise that the federally controlled naming game for radio and television stations was a very inexact process. Perhaps you could say that the naming was downright irrational. Tell me how Texas ended up with both "K" and "W" call letters, for instance.

Let's just agree that choosing call letters for radio stations often can make little sense even though the station's name turns out to be crucial to its success. One characteristic of naming certainly sticks out rather obviously: If you happen to live in a place where a radio station was started in the early 1920s, you are aware of that rare naming convention which uses only three call letters instead of four that are required today. Radio station KHJ, Los Angeles is a perfect example of a station that started in the early 1920s that was given three call letters instead of four.

Kindness, Happiness, and Joy

With a little cleverness, call letters can be chosen as an abbreviation for a thought or a sentiment. The famous call letters KHJ actually stood for Kindness, Happiness, and Joy. No, I'm not making this up!

The reputation, identity, and branding of a radio station should begin with some purposeful choice of call letters. Some famous examples of this include WGN (World's Greatest Newspaper), WSB (Welcome South, Brother) and WLS (World's Largest Store—the slogan of former owners Sears and Roebuck). One of my all-time favorite call letters is WWWW, Detroit because of simultaneous simplicity and yet difficulty to say aloud. Another is KIOI, San Francisco. Those call letters were pioneering in that the FM dial position of 101 was represented by the sequence of letters IOI.

Beyond the call letters, there are other elements that can work together to help or hinder a radio station's reputation, identity, and branding. For instance, why are most radio stations so carefully and deliberately programmed? Why not just let the person on the air say whatever he or she wants to say, and, also let them play whatever recordings they choose like in college radio?

The Business of Branding

Radio stations may <u>seem</u> to be there for the purpose of entertaining and informing you. Their true purpose, however, is that commercial radio stations exist to make money for their owners and operators by transmitting culture to audiences and informing people about what is important culturally and socially. Even noncommercial radio stations must focus upon reputation, identity, and branding, however, if they expect to survive in any highly competitive radio market regardless of its size.

To grasp how commercial radio stations can generate so much revenue for their owners and operators, one must first accept that radio programming is show business, with more of an emphasis on **business** than on show. If there is not a sufficiently appealing show, however, the business aspect will be quite difficult, if not impossible.

A radio station's reputation, identity, and brand need to achieve a top-of-mind awareness among the target audience. This is why marketing a radio station's reputation, identity, and brand occupies such a prominent role whenever a new radio format is launched on a station. I can remember from my visits to Los Angeles during my youth hearing radio stations given names with an adjective preceding the word radio.

One example I like to cite is **Color Radio**, which was coined by Chuck Blore and his associates in 1958 for KFWB radio in Hollywood. That phrase is proof of the marketing effort behind a station's reputation, identity, and brand. I respect Chuck Blore and what he accomplished. But, I think that was an odd phrase, however, to brand a radio format.

I guess I will have to admit that selecting an odd phrase as a way of branding a radio station may just make good business sense because using odd phrases seems to happen often enough. I presume that it must be okay for the strange phrase to seem illogical or otherwise disconnected from the business needs of a radio station as long as the marketing works.

Here comes the case in point that you were expecting: You might wonder why the adjective **boss** was selected in the context of naming the radio format on KHJ in 1965 in Los Angeles. Isn't the phrase **Boss Radio** strange and illogical? Yes! But, it seems that being strange and illogical can work when it comes to branding.

I recall that the word **boss** was an adjective associated in my youth with young California guys who rode surfboards on the crashing waves of the Pacific Ocean. At a very basic level, the word was a 1960s slang term used to denote the relative worth or value of something or someone.

One decade's slang probably always will differ from another's. Nobody would have imagined, for instance, that the word **bad** could morph into meaning **good** until Michael Jackson wrote and sang his famous 1987 hit song with a confusing title.

Even back in 1965, the choice of the apparently odd and not-so-logical word **boss** as an adjective to describe a radio station was unpopular. I met and interviewed people who worked at KHJ during the 1969s who did not approve of using that phrase. Rock and roll radio programmer Bill Drake was one of those people.

He told me that radio promotion man Clancy Imuslind was the person who selected the word **boss** in the early 1960s for radio station KYA, San Francisco. The marketing phrase devised KYA was **The Boss of the Bay**. You will want to read Drake's recollections about branding and other key issues in radio broadcasting presented elsewhere in this book.

By the time Boss Radio, as a brand, came to be used in Southern California in 1965 to promote KHJ, the phrase had a powerful impact: KHJ was intended to be accepted as the dominant radio station in Los Angeles, or, in other words, the boss of all LA radio stations.

A couple of well-known pop culture references come to mind that refer to the American Mafia in this same, or similar, context— *capo di tutti capi* (boss of all bosses) and *capo dei capi* (boss of bosses). But, I never heard or read anyone make such references to the KHJ or RKO Radio marketing or formats; the word **boss** in the 1960s was powerful, but not overly aggressive in the gangster context.

If nothing else is true, Boss Radio was a wise and clever choice for the marketing of KHJ, both on the air starting in 1965, and also in other promotional settings such as newspaper advertisements and at rock and roll music concerts at the Hollywood Bowl. The phrase remains as an easy-to-remember and easy-to-say symbolic reference that in the 1960s played a similar role to trademarks and domain names of the 21st century to represent or brand a positive reputation or credibility.

Astonishingly, the phrase Boss Radio was not copyrighted nor trademarked by RKO Radio during the Los Angeles marketing of the new format on KHJ. But, as you will see later in this eBook, the company that owned KHJ at that time was not the most diligent or careful corporation. So, ownership of the brand was not preserved as it could have been within a business entity. The motion picture industry in Los Angeles at that exact same time demonstrated quite well that it knew how to write contracts covering ownership of creative works, so it certainly was possible for the radio industry to do similarly. It was not possible in those days to claim legal exclusivity of the Boss Radio phrase. In fact, one AM radio station in Denver, KIMN, also chose to use the phrase for marketing that station during in the early 1960s, for example.

Protecting creative works and branding in today's world is a far more precise and serious business compared to how marketing was conducted half a century ago. Companies today go to great lengths in the legal sense to protect exclusivity in the marketing of reputation, identity, and branding.

You need look no further than Apple to find a stunning example. The Beatles once owned the famous brand for their record label and company name. After Apple of Silicon Valley fame became known for distributing content including music, this powerful California company saw the need to go to great expense to arrange a legal settlement with The Beatles and their business interests to gain exclusivity of use of the Apple brand.

Chapter 3:
The Business of Radio
Programming

You, as a listener, probably care very little about a radio station's chosen identity or brand. Like most listeners, you care very much about hearing what you want to hear when you want to hear it. The business reality is simple to express: Listener preferences drive the loyalties to particular stations that emerge in pop culture based on their on-air formats.

Properly branding a radio station is fundamental if the owners and operators of a radio station expect their station to achieve audience loyalty and ultimately, financial success. This notion dates back to the 1950s in the United States, a time when radio programming had a business need to drop the once traditional blocks of dramas, big band music, and variety programs in favor of one style of presentation formula which could fill the entire broadcast day.

Known as formula radio, this shift in conceptualizing of individual radio stations as a delivery media for a designated format forever altered the radio programming business completely.

The business need to give radio programming a new concept was specifically to avert the large losses of audience members to the new medium of television.

In 1953, Gordon McLendon's chain of radio stations became nationally distinguished because of a formulated mixture of music, news, and spirited station promotion. That year the flagship station, KLIF in Dallas, became the highest rated metropolitan station in the United States through the use of the McLendon formula for programming.

Another fabled development in the history of US radio programming history was the realization that people liked to listen repeatedly to a very limited number of songs. As the story goes, while in a bar in Omaha, Todd Storz noticed that particular jukebox selections would be repeated over and over. Since jukeboxes of that era only contained 40 single-play records, the notion of a top 40 format for radio seemed like a logical idea, so the legends has it that Storz took this concept back to his radio station WTIX in New Orleans in 1955.

To understand what radio programming formats are called, and to whom they appeal, requires understanding the overall pop culture environment. In the United States, pop culture has had a profound influence upon what listeners can hear on radio stations in major and small markets alike.

American radio programming up through the late 1940s and into the early 1950s was built out of blocks. There certainly were standouts in the pop culture sense such as Frank Sinatra, who initially attracted widespread attention for his musical genius through appearances on radio that helped drive sales of his records. But, in those days, radio stations did not emphasize music or vocalists. Stations would broadcast block segments of drama, mystery, soap opera, news, and music, both live and recorded. That so-called block programming stands in stark contrast to formula radio, which McLendon perfected in Texas and to which all radio formats since certainly owe a great debt.

This switchover to radio formats that typically center around one type of sound per radio station inevitably was linked to the advent of rock and roll music in the United States. Rock and roll music demanded to be given its own emphasis on radio stations.

Before rock and roll, listeners could expect to tune in to a radio station and hear Frank Sinatra singing one minute and then the very next thing on the air would be a radio drama. After the huge pop cultural phenomenon that rock and roll music proved to be, radio programming adapted to match both the pace and the intensity of pop culture.

There was no turning back once this pop culture shift took place. The actual birth date of rock and roll radio is disputed. However, most would probably agree with me that in the United States popular music took a giant evolutionary step as rhythm and blues mixed with country music and recording artists like Elvis Presley became the first rock and roll stars. Presley recorded his first single, *That's All Right,* in July 1954 in Memphis at the legendary Sun Studio owned and operated by Sam Phillips, guaranteeing Memphis a great and honorable benchmark in the history of rock and roll music.

Once rock and roll became started becoming commercially successful in selling records throughout the United States, stations that played only rock and roll music became quite common. The days were soon gone when most radio stations relied primarily upon block programming. The death of block programming led to other non-music radio formats, including McLendon's all-news format in 1961, his all-sports radio format, and his talk radio format.

By the mid-1960s, Los Angeles was ripe for the introduction of a new way to present rock and roll radio. The top 40 format had by then been around for a decade. The opportunity to make a change certainly had arrived.

Prior to the 1960s, KHJ did not play rock and roll music. But, in Los Angeles and elsewhere, the AM stations of that era which did play rock and roll often sounded as though they were programmed by the person who just happened to be on the air at the time.

Some stations chose to use playlists of the 40 most popular songs in deference to the well-established top 40 format. Others placed no such limits on the number of songs played. Typically, the person on the air not only could pick the music they played, but they also enjoyed the freedom to talk as much as they wanted. Fully one-third of the hour could be taken up by commercial advertisements on those stations. Music jingles on those stations often ran as long as one full minute and were embellished with lyrics that promoted the station, city, the person on the air, the weather, and what not.

The format that was named Boss Radio offered a modern sound on KHJ as an alternative to what typically was available on the air in Los Angeles and other major radio markets: Specifically, only the top-selling 30 rock and roll hits made it on the air—not the top 40. The new format allowed on-air talent only to talk over the musical introductions (or "intros") of the songs—the instrumental part before any singing begins. The musical jingles lasted only a few seconds and got quickly to the point before transitioning immediately back to another hit song. Visit www.bossradioforever.com to listen to many musical jingles used on KHJ for the new Boss Radio format and beyond. Instead of 18 minutes of commercials in any given hour, the new format presented on KHJ in 1965 cut that down to around 12 minutes maximum literally making room for "much more music," which was one of the marketing phrases used on the air in the KHJ jingles.

The emphasis upon playing much more music on rock and roll radio instead of allowing the air personalities to talk as much as they wanted is one primary reason why the new format in 1965 in Los Angeles attracted so much attention across the United States and Canada. Literally overnight, one radio station changed the presentational focus to the music and away from the person who happened to be on the air at the time.

Ironically, several of those who were selected to be on the air on KHJ in the new format distinguished themselves as radio celebrities despite the fact that the format restricted how often they could speak on the air. Notably, Robert W. Morgan and The Real Don Steele each pioneered unique and different ways to make the very best use of what little amount of time that they were given by the new format to open the microphone and their mouths.

You can listen to digital recordings of Morgan at www.robertwmorgan.com and Steele at www.reelradio.com/steele/index.html to hear how KHJ sounded. The original radio air check website www.reelradio.com is the very best place online where you can gain access to digital recordings of other radio pioneers like Bill Drake and Ron Jacobs. I also have a collection of selected audio recordings posted at www.bossradioforever.com that you may also enjoy hearing.

It Was Always About the Music

By design, the core focus of the new format that made a big ratings difference at KHJ was the *music*—not the on-air talent as the air personalities, themselves, would want you to believe. In Los Angeles during 1965 when the new format was launched on KHJ, what singer/songwriter Joni Mitchell would later call "the star-maker machinery" was in full gear. Scores of eager young men with dreams of major market stardom appeared on the new KHJ within the new format. Yet, decades later, very few names are remembered for their crucial work on that station during the late 1960s that contributed to the success of the new format.

In fact, over the years following the launch of the Boss Radio format, the lineup of on-air talent on KHJ was changed many times and often very quickly. Such is the nature of the rock and roll radio business in major markets. However, we should remember the "magnificent seven" Boss Jocks team that was assembled in Los

Angeles for the May 1965 launch of the new format on KHJ:

- Robert W. Morgan (6 to 9 am)
- Roger Christian (9 am to Noon)
- Gary Mack (Noon to 3 pm)
- The Real Don Steele (3 to 6 pm)
- Dave Diamond (6 to 9 pm)
- Sam Riddle (9 pm to Midnight)
- Johnny Williams (Overnight)

Fifty years ago, there were no females admitted to the ranks of on-air radio personalities. Woman were stuck in administrative jobs only in those days. And just try finding any people of color chosen during the 1960s for regular shifts as on-air talent on Los Angeles radio stations with the highest ratings.

Quite simply, the single most important aspect about Boss Radio KHJ was the music. A very high output of the Southern California-based recording industry product in those days coincided with the arrival of the new format on KHJ. So many unforgettable recording artists were consistently producing and releasing new rock and roll music at that time. Their timely product was showcased on Boss Radio KHJ. The legacies of successful recording artists such as The Beach Boys, The Beatles, Cher, Marvin Gaye, Dianna Ross, The Rolling Stones, and Stevie Wonder—whose songs were popularized on the new KHJ in the

1960s—and have continued in popularity well into the 21ˢᵗ century.

The Hits Just Keep on Comin'

Here are the number one songs played on Boss Radio KHJ in the 1960s after the station had become LA's most popular station but before FM radio became the dominant medium for rock and roll music starting in the 1970s:

—1966—

Just Like Me—Paul Revere & The Raiders

These Boots Are Made For Walkin—Nancy Sinatra

California Dreamin'—Mamas & Papas

Soul And Inspiration—Righteous Brothers

Bang Bang—Cher

Monday, Monday—Mamas & Papas

When A Man Loves A Woman—Percy Sledge

A Groovy Kind Of Love—Mindbenders

Searching For My Love—Bobby Moore

Strangers In The Night—Frank Sinatra

Lil' Red Riding Hood—Sam The Sham & The Pharaohs

Summer In The City—The Lovin' Spoonful

Sunny—Bobby Hebb

Yellow Submarine / Eleanor Rigby—The Beatles

You Can't Hurry Love—The Supremes

Cherish—The Association

Psychotic Reaction—Count Five 96 Tears—? & The Mysterians

I'm Your Puppet—James & Bobby Purify

Good Vibrations—The Beach Boys

Devil With A Blue Dress On &Good Golly Miss Molly—Mitch
Ryder & The Detroit Wheels

I'm A Believer / Steppin' Stone—The Monkees

—1967—

Ruby Tuesday—The Rolling Stones

Happy Together—The Turtles

Then You Can Tell Me Goodbye—The Casinos

There's A Kind Of Hush / No Milk Today—Herman's Hermits

Somethin' Stupid—Nancy & Frank Sinatra

I Think We're Alone Now—Tommy James & The Shondells

The Happening—The Supremes

Groovin'—The Young Rascals

Society's Child—Janis Ian

Light My Fire—The Doors

The Oogum Boogum Song—Brenton Wood

I Was Made To Love Her—Stevie Wonder

Can't Take My Eyes Off You—Frankie Valli

All You Need Is Love / Baby You're A Rich Man—The Beatles

San Franciscan Nights—The Animals

Ode To Billie Joe—Bobbie Gentry

The Letter—Box Tops

Apples, Peaches, Pumpkin Pie—Jay & The Techniques

Higher And Higher—Jackie Wilson

How Can I Be Sure—The Rascals

It Must Be Him—Vicki Carr

Expressway To Your Heart—Soul Survivors

I Say A Little Prayer—Dionne Warwick

Different Drum—Stone Poneys

I Second That Emotion—The Miracles

Hello Goodbye / I Am The Walrus—The Beatles

Boogaloo Down Broadway—Fantastic Johnny C

Itchycoo Park—Small Faces

—1968—

Spooky—Classics IV

Nobody But Me—Human Beinz

Green Tambourine—Lemon Pipers

Love Is Blue—Paul Mauriat

The Dock Of The Bay—Otis Redding

(Theme From) Valley Of The Dolls—Dionne Warwick

Mighty Quinn—Manfred Mann

Young Girl—Gary Puckett & The Union Gap

Cry Like A Baby—Box Tops

Honey—Bobby Goldsboro

A Beautiful Morning—The Rascals

The Good, The Bad And The Ugly—Hugo Montenegro

Tighten Up—Archie Bell & The Drells

This Guy's In Love With You—Herb Alpert

Mony Mony—Tommy James & The Shondells

Jumpin' Jack Flash—The Rolling Stones

Hurdy Gurdy Man—Donovan

Grazing In The Grass—Hugh Masekela

Hello, I Love You—The Doors

Classical Gas—Mason Williams

People Got To Be Free—The Rascals

Born To Be Wild—Steppenwolf

On The Road Again—Canned Heat

Harper Valley P.T.A.—Jeannie C. Riley

Hey Jude / Revolution—The Beatles

Girl Watcher—O'Kaysions

Those Were The Days—Mary Hopkin

Magic Carpet Ride—Steppenwolf

Love Child—The Supremes

Stormy—Classics IV

For Once In My Life—Stevie Wonder

Lo Mucho Que Te Quiero—Rene & Rene

I Heard It Through The Grapevine—Marvin Gaye

Soulful Strut—Young-Holt Unlimited

—1969—

Crimson And Clover—Tommy James & The Shondells

Everyday People—Sly & The Family Stone

You Showed Me—The Turtles

Mendocino—Sir Douglas Quintet

Baby, Baby Don't Cry—Miracles

Traces—Classics IV

Indian Giver—1910 Fruitgum Co.

Time Of The Season—Zombies

Dizzy—Tommy Roe

Aquarius / Let The Sunshine In— The Fifth Dimension

More Today Than Yesterday—Spiral Staircase

Hair—The Cowsills

Oh Happy Day—Edwin Hawkins Singers

Bad Moon Rising—Creedence Clearwater Revival

Grazing In The Grass—Friends Of Distinction

Love Theme From Romeo & Juliet—Henry Mancini

What Does It Take (To Win Your Love)—Jr. Walker & The All Stars

Crystal Blue Persuasion—Tommy James & The Shondells

My Cherie Amour—Stevie Wonder

In The Year 2525—Zager & Evans

Ruby, Don't Take Your Love To Town—First Edition

A Boy Named Sue—Johnny Cash

Honky Tonk Women—The Rolling Stones

Sugar, Sugar—The Archies

Easy To Be Hard—Three Dog Night

Hurt So Bad—The Lettermen

Oh, What A Night—The Dells

Little Woman—Bobby Sherman

Suspicious Minds—Elvis Presley

Hot Fun In The Summertime—Sly & The Family Stone

Take A Letter Maria—R.B. Greaves

Something / Come Together—The Beatles

Someday We'll Be Together—The Supremes

Raindrops Keep Fallin' On My Head—B.J. Thomas

The question needs to be asked: Did the music played within the new format on Boss Radio KHJ make the format and the station so successful? Or, was it the other way around? Was Boss Radio KHJ a channel for the transmission of pop culture? Or could pop culture have been transmitted to the people in some other way without this radio station?

In the 1960s one radio station in one American city could more easily distinguish itself from all the rest across an entire nation compared to today when that accomplishment would be almost impossible. For one thing, in those days there were far fewer radio stations on the air than we have today. There were also many more mom-and-pop owners of radio stations in contrast to today's mega corporation control of radio stations in many markets across the United States.

As the Elton John hit *Crocodile Rock* asks, "Do you remember when rock was young?" The year 1965 was that time. It was the first full year after The Beatles initially came to the United States, and the entire recorded music industry on both sides of the Atlantic was supercharged by a high-energy competition between British and American rock and roll music artists.

This made the mid-1960s a major turning point for rock and roll music, which during this particular time became big business for major record labels that wanted to cash in on the exploding audience interest. The new format on Boss Radio KHJ was launched within this social and economic context in Los Angeles, a nexus for the North American record labels.

Who would have noticed, for instance, if this rock and roll radio approach had been launched anywhere else but in the entertainment capital of the world? Common sense told me that it would be very difficult to accomplish the same or similar kind of financial success of this rock and roll radio format had the format been rolled out on AM radio in any other market than Los Angeles. I posed this question to Bill Drake, asking whether he thought that there was something inherent in California that allowed for growth in the creative sense in radio programming as compared to other states.

Drake, who was from the state of Georgia, said, "I think that Boston and Detroit are pretty much like LA as far as operating a [rock and roll radio] station. I think it wouldn't have made a whole lot of difference [had Boss Radio started in the east instead of in the west]. I'll tell you this: I sure as hell would rather have been living here and going to New York from time to time than living in New York and going anywhere. I'm sure that if I'd lived in New York at the time, I'd probably have been on the road 300 days a year."

What about the differences between radio programming in Los Angeles versus San Francisco? After the success of the Boss Radio format in Los Angeles on KHJ in 1965, the parent company (RKO) had Drake and company bring the same sound to San Francisco on KFRC.

Prior to making a success of the Boss Radio format in Los Angeles, Drake had previously worked in San Francisco, so he had a high familiarity with all that was San Francisco radio in the 1960s.

One well known and uniquely San Francisco style or sound belonged to Tom Donahue in the 1960s. Drake told me that he knew Donahue quite well. "We were doing two different things," Drake said. "Donahue and I had worked together at KYA. When I was program director at KYA, he was a jock there, and a damn good one." Drake explained to me that the trade magazines' commentary in those days about Donahue's "aesthetic appreciation" of music programming versus Drake's "product oriented" approach was a mischaracterization. Drake said, "I don't think that I could ever try to explain away what I did by saying I was doing it for art's sake. That's bullshit. I think that anybody in this business who says they are—I don't care if they're a liquor company or a radio station or whether they are an artist or [musical] group or anything–anyone who says they're doing it for art's sake is either lying or a failure, one of the two."

Clearly, what Drake did for radio programming was not about art for art's sake. Rather, the sum total of what Drake did for radio programming was always all about reaching Drake's own extremely high professional standards. Drake's business partner,

Gene Chenault (pronounced shuh NAULT), provided for me a unique inside view about how he evaluated his partner, the legendary radio programmer: "Drake is so much of a perfectionist that he is sometimes unhappy because perfection is not easily attained," Chenault told me.

Let me conclude here with a brief sketch of the connection of culture and radio programming over the decades since the launch of the Boss Radio format.

1960s

The youthful John Fitzgerald Kennedy was elected 35th president of the United States in 1960 demonstrating a new way of thinking: It was possible for young people to have dreams to grow up and lead the world. The rock and roll radio efforts that Drake-Chenault led in California in the early 1960s happened in this exact social context—a time during which people believed that almost anything could be accomplished if you only set your sights high enough. If nothing else is true, the people responsible for the rock and roll sound on Boss Radio in Los Angeles saw themselves as young and visionary.

Meanwhile, the presidency of JFK—described as "Camelot" with an exaggerated legendary, fabled air—got into trouble. A botched invasion of Cuba in 1961 at the Bay of Pigs showed a surprising vulnerability of the U.S. military. But in 1962, however,

JFK demonstrated extreme presidential machismo by ordering a military blockade of Cuba even while the action skirted the very edge of world war.

In August 1963, the civil rights movement in the U.S. achieved a new momentum when the reverend Dr. Martin Luther King, Jr. gave his "I Have A Dream" speech in Washington, DC. Four months later, JFK was shot dead while riding in an open car motorcade on the streets of Dallas, Texas. Rock and roll radio in those days had a difficult time trying to put this shocking event into perspective amid the emphasis on musical entertainment.

Beginning in late 1963, the nation's sensibilities were suddenly shifted. JFK was buried at Arlington National Cemetery beneath an eternal flame. Lyndon Baines Johnson became president and ultimately signed into law the Civil Rights Act that JFK had championed.

In a major cultural shift, the American rock and roll music scene was jolted in 1964 as The Beatles arrived, forever altering how both radio/television broadcasting and the recorded music industry handles rock and roll.

That same year, an African-American man from Louisville, Kentucky who took the Islamic name of Muhammad Ali became the World Heavyweight Champion. The usually controversial Ali proved to be one of the greatest American athletes of the 20th century. In so doing, he drew attention to the Black Muslims in the United States. In early 1965, Malcom X, an African-American Islamic leader who announced his belief that there could be brotherhood between black and white, was assassinated in New York City.

And there was warfare. Washington, DC in early 1965 saw the first major rally to protest the U.S. military efforts in Southeast Asia, which was becoming the most significant blemish upon the Lyndon Johnson presidency.

In Los Angeles, a few months after Boss Radio brought financial success to KHJ, intense pressures created by racial prejudice continued to build in Southern California.

The concept of a black radio personality entertaining listeners of all races had not yet arrived back then. Boss Radio regularly played hit music of black entertainers. The very first song played on KHJ when Boss Radio launched was Dancing in the Streets by Martha Reeves and the Vandellas. This, and other, popular Motown hits were often played on 93/KHJ. But otherwise, Boss Radio essentially was all-white, and except for behind-the-scenes music and administrative people, was all-male.

As KHJ grew in popularity in Southern California during the summer of 1965, racial tensions heated up until early August of that year when a white police officer arrested a black man for drunk driving, sparking six days of rioting in the Watts section of Los Angeles that ended the lives of 34 people.

A conservative shift in California politics immediately followed the LA riots. A most notable impact was conservative Republican Ronald Reagan's rise in popularity. Reagan blamed the riots on the incumbent governor, liberal Democrat Edmond G. "Pat" Brown (the father of Jerry Brown, California governor from 2011 - 2018). Ronald Reagan unseated Pat Brown to became the governor of California—an essential stepping stone to his two terms as President of the United States, 1981-1989.

The year 1966 saw the establishment of the Black Panther Party. Ever larger protests were mounted against the federal policy of drafting young men into U.S. military service in Southeast Asia. And just when it seemed that the nation would implode from prejudice and protests, in 1966 the original Star Trek television series premiered with its sci-fi stories about the value of diversity. The series was filmed in Hollywood at Desilu studios (now Paramount Pictures) on Melrose Avenue next door to KHJ.

In June 1967, The Beatles released 40 minutes of music that changed radio and records forever. *Sgt. Pepper's Lonely Hearts Club Band* set very high standards against which all rock and roll performers will be measured. It was the first time anyone had deliberately put songs together in a particular order on one rock and roll album with little or no spaces between tracks to create a unified listener experience.

Rock and roll AM radio stations at the time mainly played many different songs each hour-none of which lasted more than about three and one-half minutes. The then-new FM radio with stereo sound and no static embraced a less structured format that allowed longer songs, so this meant that the Sgt. Pepper album's music was aired mainly on FM stations. This one album signaled the beginning of the end of AM radio's dominance in rock and roll radio.

Also significant was the psychedelic nature of Sgt. Pepper precisely at a time when the recreational use of drugs was rippling through U.S. culture. Timothy Leary, a psychology professor at Harvard, became the outspoken advocate of mind-altering drugs like LSD and others. The popular music of the time reflected the undercurrent of recreational drug use. Boss Radio KHJ and other RKO radio stations in those days regularly played songs by artists like The Beatles, The Doors, The Rolling Stones and others who did not complete conceal the influences of recreational drug use upon their art.

During this era, it may have seemed as though U.S. culture was trending toward more tolerance of violence. The manner in which violence appeared in society and culture changed rapidly as major motion pictures from this time period such as *Bonnie and Clyde* and *The Wild Bunch* radically shifted the public's sensibilities regarding blood and death as portrayed on the silver screen.

But, blood wasn't just in the movies. During the late 1960s violence was, indeed, increasing in real life. Dr. Martin Luther King, Jr. was gunned down in Memphis in April 1968. Riots erupted immediately in Washington, DC and other major U.S. cities. Because of social unrest in the United States created on two fronts-by racial tensions and also by protests against the war in Southeast Asia-in early 1968, President Lyndon Johnson shocked the nation by announcing he would not run again.

New York Senator Robert Francis Kennedy—brother of the late president John F. Kennedy—emerged as the apparent frontrunner for the presidency in 1968. But, just minutes after RFK made his Los Angeles victory speech in the California presidential primary, he was shot and died the next day. KHJ staff members were deeply affected by the assassination for several reasons, but chief among them was the fact that the Los Angeles campaign headquarters for RFK had been across the street from the KHJ studios.

A few weeks later, the assassination of RFK was a contributing factor to the violent riots that disrupted the Democratic National Convention in Chicago in full view of continuous, live network television coverage. In November of that year, Richard Nixon, pledging to bring order to a troubled nation, was elected the 37th president. He took office in January 1969. It proved to be a complex year during which gay rights made it onto the national radar screen following the Stonewall Bar riot in New York City; the United States finally beat the Russians by being first to succeed at a manned landing on the moon; and a frustrated would-be rock star named Charles Manson perpetrated a grizzly mass murder in Los Angeles.

As Star Trek said would happen, human exploration of space exploration becomes a reality. In July 1969, the United States of America wins the space race with the Russians by successfully completing the first human mission to the moon and back to our planet.

1970s

When the new decade began, protests against the U.S. military efforts in Southeast Asia intensified. A riot near the University of California at Santa Barbara destroyed a branch of Bank of America, and in Ohio, four students attending Kent State University were shot dead by national guard troops during an antiwar protest. It began to seem that the war in Southeast Asia would bring down Richard Nixon as it had Lyndon Johnson.

Instead, a break-in at the Watergate complex along the Potomac River in Washington, DC led to the self-destruction of the Nixon presidency. Although Nixon ran for re-election in 1972 and won, he abruptly resigned the presidency to avoid being impeached in 1974.

Throughout these eventful years, the Drake-Chenault programming evolved from KHJ in Los Angeles and Boss Radio (a brand name that ultimately appeared on other radio stations) to a national syndicated radio programming effort using reels of recorded tape. The invention of the digital compact disc—the CD—like Sgt. Pepper's Lonely Hearts Club Band before, would revolutionize the radio and record business once again. Eventually, radio stations would switch entirely to playing music on CD and the era of vinyl disks on the radio was almost entirely over.

As a reward for how well KHJ performed in the Los Angeles ratings, RKO General signed the Drake-Chenault team to program AM stations in San Francisco, Detroit, Boston, Memphis, and WOR-FM in New York City with derivations of the Boss Radio format. Drake and Chenault expanded their reach outside of the RKO chain of stations. A national radio programming syndication company was formed (eventually named Drake-Chenault Enterprises) to provide FM stations with high-quality programming using prerecorded audio tape programs. In so doing, Drake-Chenault Enterprises played a central role in permanently establishing FM as the dominant radio medium for rock and roll music in the U.S., edging out AM once and for all.

But, RKO General was not happy to watch Drake-Chenault Enterprises grow while the ratings of RKO stations began to drop. So, in 1973 RKO ended its contract with the Drake-Chenault team. After six months waiting out the noncompete clause in their RKO contract, Drake and Chenault began a five-year contract programming FM station K100 in Hollywood with yet another derivation of their famous format. However, the Drake-Chenault programming failed to turn K100 into a ratings success. Various other formats were attempted, including semi- and fully-automated varieties from companies such as Transtar.

1980s

Ronald Reagan was president of the United States for most of the decade. Ownership restrictions of radio and television stations continued to weaken at the Federal Communications Commission under a Republican-dominated Congress. K100 was ultimately purchased by Westwood One and the station became KQLZ, "Pirate Radio." In 1989 Jones Intercable entered into a partnership with what was then called Drake-Chenault Radio Consultants to create Jones Radio Networks. One of the biggest changes in popular culture came in the 1980s when video killed the radio star:

Music programming on the radio received a formidable challenge with the advent of music videos shown nationally on Music Television MTV.

1990s

The 25th anniversary of Boss Radio KHJ in 1990 was the very last time that the radio pioneers and their entire team celebrated a reunion together. The Drake-Chenault taped syndicated radio programming business was sold by Jones in 1991 to Broadcast Programming in Seattle. At that same time, Jones bought out the remaining interest Drake-Chenault had in Jones Radio Networks and the famous hyphenated brand name Drake-Chenault was no more.

The FCC rules on station ownership are changed in the late 1990s during the presidency of William Jefferson Clinton. Some credit or blame the Republican-controlled Congress of the United States for sweeping changes in ownership that result in concentrating most U.S. radio stations under the control of a few huge corporations like Clear Channel.

The late 1990s also were a time when hip hop grew from a strictly New York City neighborhoods cultural phenomenon of the 1970s to a cultural force that swept across the entire U.S. Just like rock and roll music in the 1950s and 1960s had done, hip hop in 1990s forcefully and similarly changed the U.S. music entertainment industry and radio programming as well. At roughly the same time, the internet emerged as a potentially revolutionary new communications technology.

2000s

The first decade of the 21st century proven to be a time of tumultuous change in the U.S. that was similar in its cultural impact to the time period of the late 1960s. War in Southeast Asia was the political focal point of the late 1960s. After the 2001 terrorist attacks upon New York City and the Pentagon, war in Iraq during that decade held a similarly powerful significance upon life and culture in the U.S.

The cultural ripple effect of the 9/11 terrorist attacks included outspoken protests by entertainment and music industry celebrities to the subsequent warfare in, and military occupation of, Iraq by the U.S. As in the late 1960s and early 1970s, when the U.S. military endeavors in Southeast Asia prompted movies and music that presented opinions about political and military events, the early 21st century war in Iraq has led to equivalent popular culture expressions.

There were antiwar protest songs showing up on the Billboard music charts during the U.S. military involvement in Southeast Asia, mainly in the form of rock and roll as well as folk music. In the 2000s, however, Billboard charted music that offered commentary about the U.S. military involvement in Iraq from within country and hip hop songs.

At this same time, the internet grew in popularity in the U.S. and around the world. This enabled rapid and hugely influential changes in technology such as downloadable music that is playable on hand-held phones. The methods of transmitting popular culture in the U.S. and around the world keeps changing decade to decade. Once viable retail sales of popular music on CD faced serious financial challenges in the U.S. and led to the closing down of influential retail music businesses such as Tower Records. Hip hop on the radio and in downloadable forms enjoyed a tremendous financial growth and eclipsed the pop culture power of rock and roll on the radio.

The British invasion of U.S. popular culture in the 1960s was accomplished by rock and roll artists like the Beatles and the Rolling Stones, who relied upon radio programming in the U.S. to drive the sales of their music. In the 2000s, a second successful British invasion of U.S. popular culture was launched. Simon Cowell and other producers from the U.K. have overwhelmingly addicted U.S. audiences to American Idol, a star-maker vehicle using prime-time television programming to generate significant revenue from the sales of recorded music.

2010s

The second decade of the 21st century was no less tumultuous when considering the popular culture impact of changing technology. Facebook hit 400 million active users in 2010 on the way to the 2017 milestone of 1.94 billion. This sheer power in numbers is why Facebook became the single most influential transmitter of popular culture on Earth. How can any one individual terrestrial radio station ever hope to compete with that?

The internet, itself, continued its cultural ripple effect around the world that started back in the mid-1990s. The faster speeds that were developed and popularized during this second decade helped stimulate the everyday routine of worldwide sharing of files containing both music and video at levels that during the 1980s MTV would never have dreamed were possible. Self-distributing of digital products and brands is now commonplace for budding international talents without the need to go through the gatekeeping processes of the traditional corporate-controlled channels from the 20th century.

Chapter 4:
Bad Karma on Sunset Boulevard

In 1972, four businessmen—W. John Driscoll, John J. Pascoe, Edward L. Scarff, and Wayne K. Van Dyck—together purchased the 58,000-watt KFOX-FM in Los Angeles. This turns out to be the very Los Angeles FM station where my college radio friend, who became known on the air on Hollywood radio as "Hurricane Hines," helped me get hired. So began my career adventure in major market radio.

Since the station's frequency was 100.3 MHz, there emerged a marketing opportunity to promote the numeral "100" as the core brand. San Francisco broadcasting pioneer James Gabbert had already proved the promotional value of conveying the dial position of a radio station through call letters. His influential FM station was promoted as K101. Since call letters do not allow numerals, Gabbert had to choose an equivalent using only letters of the alphabet. So, he chose KIOI for his call letters. The letter "I" stood for the numeral "1" and the letter "O" stood for zero. The result was the legal station identification that was spoken aloud as "kay-eye-oh-eye, San Francisco." Station identification on K101 often included an overdubbed voice that said "one-oh-one" aloud simultaneously with "eye-oh-eye" enabling the clever and constantly reinforced brand over the air.

That same idea was emulated in Los Angeles to rebrand the former KFOX-FM. To promote the FM dial position at 100, the need was to find call letters that would convey or suggest the number 100. The first choice was to have the call letters be KIOO since the "I" could be a "1" and the "OO" could be "00" but those call letters were already taken. Plan "B" was to go with an "I" followed by "QQ" so the letters "IQQ" could suggest "100." Of course, pronouncing the call letters KIQQ aloud as "kay-eye-cue-cue" would never suggest "K100," so the station was promoted as "kay-one-hundred" and "kay-eye-cue-cue" was reserved only for the purposes of the legal station identification at the top of each hour.

The company name chosen by the KIQQ owners was Cosmic Communications. On my very first visit to the station, I was surprised to see that someone obviously had hired some "hip and groovy" 1970s designer to "do" the look of the offices and studios. The custom logo featured prominent, stylized bolts of bright yellow lightning. There were painted stars in a celestial panorama depicting an endless cosmos wallpapered across much of the surface area of the walls.

This odd choice would have been fine, except that those cartoonish lightning bolts popped up everywhere as if the designer was expressing mockery of power versus respect for power. And, one couldn't escape the metaphorical irony: While Cosmic K100 had high-energy lightning bolts seemingly everywhere on the walls of its offices and studios that suggested strong flashiness and boldness, on the air, the station had a very relaxed and mellow sound that included music from Johnny Mathis and The Carpenters along with Lou Reed and The Beatles. This soft rock sound mix was new in the early 1970s and the format attracted a loyal, yet small audience. But, high-energy lightning bolts seemed completely wrong as a visual metaphor for the KIQQ facilities.

Unfortunately, the financial success of KIQQ was hampered by technology. The signal transmitted from the Santa Monica Mountains was insufficiently powerful to blanket the entire Los Angeles radio market. The successful FM stations of that time all had transmitters atop the landmark Mount Wilson, which has an elevation of almost a mile above sea level in the San Gabriel Mountains. The format also proved to be a business problem. Soft rock as a format in the early 1970s certainly may have been ahead of its time, but the mellow blend of current hits, recent favorites, and oldies, intended to be an alternative to rock and roll stations in LA, could not attain financial success like the owners wanted. This format on FM ultimately proved to be a ratings winner in various major markets, but not in 1972 and not on KIQQ in Los Angeles.

Razor Blade Censorship

There also were some downright peculiar decisions made about the music played on the Cosmic K100. I admit here with major shame that as the one who handled production, I reported to a program director who told me I was required to edit *Stairway to Heaven* by Led Zeppelin before that hit song was allowed on the air. Like nobody would notice!

My defense is the truth: ***I was only following orders***.

If I wanted to keep my job at that Hollywood radio station, I had no choice but to use a razor blade to slash away the very guts of *Stairway to Heaven*—arguably one of the most famous and influential rock and roll songs of all time.

I believe that horrendous Cosmic K100 edited version of *Stairway to Heaven* without the Jimmie Page guitar solo certainly brought on some seriously bad karma for the radio station. I could not shake the feeling at the time that my senseless butchery of that classic rock and roll song deeply infuriated the show biz gods who lived in another dimension within the star-studded walls of the KIQQ offices and studios. Sometimes, late at night, I felt what could only be described as "a weird vibe" inside the offices and studios of the station. I concluded that those deities no doubt exacted a fitting retribution for my slicing and dicing of that Led Zeppelin song: I believed that the show biz gods doomed this particular radio station frequency at 100.3 MHz in Los Angeles to failure.

High Points at a Doomed Radio Station

If I switch to looking on the brighter side, my adventures in LA radio had a few high points, too. The studios and offices of the utterly doomed radio station happened to be located in the Los Angeles community known as Hollywood on a street you just may have heard of: **Sunset Boulevard**. There just are no words that can adequately describe how thrilled I was to be working on that street in the fabled land of my childhood fantasies. Wow, to be twenty-something in Hollywood, and to be employed entertaining a radio audience was a stunning experience for me as a young man. I just kept on denying to myself that I had brought a curse upon the station, and I buried deep me the psychic feeling that persisted in warning me to expect my time at KIQQ to be short!

I chose to make every second count that I had there at that radio station. One sunny weekend, my paternal grandfather, who at that time was in his 70s, came with my parents to visit me in Los Angeles. Clearly, this visit was so that my parents could "check up on me" because I was known for seldom calling or writing home. My grandfather, Tony Goulart, was very "old school" literally because he had come to California from the old country, the Azores Islands of Portugal.

I did not get the impression that my grandfather thought favorably about my choice to work in the radio broadcasting business in comparison to him—a man of the earth who had made a living off the land, working with his hands. Well, the truth is Tony Goulart gained wealth through owning and selling land. This man was someone I preferred to steer clear of because he always seemed to me way too serious and grandfatherly. But, there I was one morning in Hollywood on Sunset Boulevard with a classic disapproving grandfather standing next to me in the production room at KIQQ. The view looking east out of the huge windows from that upper floor of the high-rise office building was nothing short of spectacular. We could easily see the snow-capped peak of Mount Baldy in the Angeles National Forest some 50 miles or so away from Hollywood. Tony Goulart made eye contact with me for a moment, conveying a clear sense that he had not expected his first grandchild to end up literally in high places. I can go back in my mind to that precious moment in time whenever I need to boost my self-esteem. That is precisely the kind of moment in a person's life that, if it were depicted in an Andrew Lloyd Webber musical, there would now be a celebratory and triumphant song.

As exciting as my life already had become at this cursed Hollywood radio station on Sunset Boulevard, I soon entered darker, uncharted territory: The four owners of KIQQ responded to the unspectacular ratings earned by the soft-rock format by signing Bill Drake and his business partner Lester Eugene ("Gene") Chenault in 1973 to a management contract. This contract gave Drake and Chenault control over programming, commercial time sales, and general management of KIQQ, which they immediately rebranded as "the new K100" after deciding to retain KIQQ, Los Angeles as the legal call letters and station identification.

When a radio station's ratings disappoint the owners and stockholders, one very predictable outcome is the immediate terminations of almost everybody who works at the station. This is one of the basic facts of life if you choose to remain in the risky business that is radio broadcasting.

In San Francisco there was a stunning mass termination just before Christmas in 2011 that gutted radio station KGO. Several famous talk radio hosts were fired after working for three decades on the air at KGO. Merry Christmas and you're all fired. Perhaps Hallmark might produce a holiday card to express that timeless sentiment.

The practice of mass terminations in the broadcasting industry may make any sensible person stop and think carefully about aiming for a career in such an unpredictable business. On the other hand, there are those very insightful *No Business Like Show Business* lyrics from Irving Berlin to explain once and for all this madness of choosing to work in total unpredictability and insecurity: "Even with a turkey that you know will fold. You may get stranded out in the cold. Still you wouldn't trade it for a sack of gold. Let's go on with the show!"

The prospect of getting fired has always been a part of the essential fabric of the broadcasting industry. When the Drake-Chenault team took over at KIQQ in December 1973, I was expecting to be let go. I watched as others were called into an office, one by one, and told that they had to leave immediately. But, somehow, one bookkeeper and I—the actual person who had been the instrument of the bad karma on Sunset Boulevard for this condemned radio station—were kept on as employees. This unexpected outcome set in motion a whole new series of career adventures for me in LA radio.

So, why were the two of us kept at KIQQ? Keeping the bookkeeper made sense to me. She knew all the essential financial information to operate the radio station. But, me? I was suspicious that the show biz gods, who were going to destroy me, first would fuck with my sanity.

But, since I knew how to operate all the production and broadcasting equipment, keeping me on at least temporarily made sense. My technical knowledge and expertise turned out to be helpful at the station under the new management since the on-air staff—notably, Robert W. Morgan and The Real Don Steele—had primarily worked for years in a union shop environment where they were prohibited by union regulations from operating the broadcasting equipment. Yet, because they had many years of actual hands-on radio experience prior to working in Hollywood at 93/KHJ, Morgan and Steele quickly learned how to operate the broadcasting equipment at KIQQ. This would come to mean that my services as an employee at KIQQ were not going to be needed for very long.

Chapter 5:
Sex, Drugs, and Rock and Roll

No exploration into rock and roll radio would be complete without some obligatory reference to sex and drugs. These three things, of course, are presumed to go together well. *Tres bien ensemble.* So, here we go: I arrived in Los Angeles to work at KIQQ when I was age 22. As with any young male at that particular age, I was, as the cliché says, "young, dumb, and full of cum."

My first night as a full-time employee in LA radio turned out to lack all the glitz and glamour that I had fantasized I would find if only I somehow could relocate away from the sleepy little town of San Luis Obispo. I guess I dreamed about what every young male would dream about who got the chance to work in Hollywood: I expected to find physical and emotional and career fulfillment—not necessarily in that specific order.

Crime and Punishment

After working my first day on the job in Hollywood at KIQQ, I came face to face with "big-city" crime. Somebody broke into my

1970 Volkswagen Beetle and stole my radio—a very cheap AM/FM receiver that I'm sure cost no more than $25 at that time. I had legally put my VW inside the multistory parking garage behind 6430 Sunset Boulevard, where the KIQQ radio station offices and studios were located.

The Hollywood police station at 1358 Wilcox Avenue turned out to be just a few blocks away. That building would be immortalized in mid-1970s television shows such as *Starsky and Hutch*, but in 1972, it was unknown to me as such a newcomer to the LA basin.

Because the police station was so near to the radio station, it wasn't long before a squad car arrived in response to my call. I would add here that the response time to emergency calls in 1972 was far faster than what one might expect today.

The cop who stepped out of the squad car was a vivid stereotype from the television cop shows of that era—a lot of muscles, blond hair and blue eyes. As Hollywood's own Hurricane Hines, a new radio personality in town, and I stood in that crunchy windshield glass on the parking garage floor next to my VW, the blond cop asked us, "Didn't I arrest you two guys earlier this week for pimping on La Cienega?"

It took me awhile to process what that question meant because I was from a small town. But, it finally sunk in what the Hollywood policeman was insinuating: That cop saw Hurricane Hines and I as the types of guys who could sell themselves as sex objects!

After all my incessant fantasizing from the safety of San Luis Obispo about finding physical fulfillment in Tinsel town, there I was being characterized by a Hollywood law enforcement official as someone who could commit sex crimes in Los Angeles! Wow, my street credibility seemed to shoot sky high that night. Thanks to my excitement over being transformed suddenly into a Southern California sex criminal, I completely forgot about the theft of that cheap car radio.

Perhaps Hurricane Hines and I were guys who had faces for radio, as the cliché says. I'm very sure that the muscular blond cop was more likely than us to succeed in selling himself for sex on La Cienega Boulevard if he had chosen to take a walk on the wild side.

The fantasizing about what I would find in LA radio turned out to be frustrating for me. First and foremost, in the sexual sense, I came to a rather sudden acceptance that what I could imagine happening to me sexually in Hollywood probably was only in my mind. That was my punishment, or so I thought, for having dare to fantasize.

Certifiable Hollywood Sex Criminal

But, wait! There's more: After I was on the air on KIQQ for a little while, it was only a matter of time before I started to receive telephone calls from female listeners who wanted much more than to request a song. I eventually relented after one particular woman persisted. I agreed to meet her out in real life instead of hiding behind the anonymity afforded by a radio microphone in a studio somewhere many stories above ground level in Hollywood.

I don't mean to suggest that I perceived of myself as being unattractive. In those days, I was 6-foot 4 and had bushy hair that I had been told by various women made me look sexy.

When you're on the radio, listeners will make a judgment about you based on the sound of your voice and your personality. They cannot see whether you've got sexy hair or if you are tall and sexually desirable.

So, the evening finally arrived when I was to meet this woman with whom I had only spoken by telephone. The standard pre-date

questions ("what do you look like?" and "what do you like to do?")
had already taken place over the telephone before we met.

I don't remember if I repeated the endorsements that I had
received about my bushy, sexy hair. I suppose I said to her on the
phone, "I'm tall, dark, and I like Mexican food." Such an idiotic
response!

She likely would have concluded that I was Hispanic. Not that
it would have had a problem with being thought of as Hispanic; I
just had spent most of my life arguing with people who assumed
my being of Portuguese heritage meant that I was Hispanic.
Perhaps I could have impressed her if only I had cited that
Hollywood cop's assessment me as some guy who could sell his
body for sex on the street. Or, I maybe that would have driven her
away very quickly.

My problems with her began the moment that I labeled her
merely as a groupie. Well, that's an eye-opener, now isn't it?

In the 1970s, every red-blooded male who listened to rock and
roll knew what a groupie was. We all had read descriptions in
Rolling Stone about this celebrity or that celebrity attracting
groupies like flames attract moths. I just never envisioned myself
as being sufficiently sexually indiscriminate like rock and roll
stars, who apparently can jump into exchanging bodily fluids with

anyone who will worship them. During my fantasizing from the aforementioned slow town, my imagined physical fulfillment did not include encounters with complete strangers as the desired path to orgasmic release. I'm sure that I was sufficiently naïve to have imagined as I did that in Los Angeles I would meet my soul mate before getting to intercourse. No doubt this kind of utterly imbecilic view of sexual activity is what should best be expected if, like me, you experienced a Roman Catholic education from grade one through twelve!

So, here's the plan that the groupie and I agreed upon: We would arrive separately to meet and dine together at a designated restaurant on Santa Monica Boulevard and then we would go to a Los Angeles Lakers game at the Fabulous Forum in Inglewood. I cannot remember what the dollar value of my date with the groupie was, but I believe that buying two Lakers tickets would not have been cheap by the standards in those days. The restaurant probably was a Marie Callender's, so trust me, I did not view this entire evening a high-ticket way to get someone into bed.

Meeting and interacting with her was, to put it bluntly, quite awkward. I felt like I was way out of my element, whatever my element actually was in those days. She responded to me like I was the most attractive fellow that she had ever met in all of Los Angeles. The way she looked at me communicated volumes about how much she wanted to get horizontal with me without clothing as fast as humanly possible.

Of course, I did not find her the least bit attractive sexually. Not surprisingly, some of my fellow would-be radio celebrities back at KIQQ had urged me in advance to go as far as I could with this groupie. My mind raced as I tried to concoct some credible falsehoods that I would be able to share with them the following morning. I desperately needed to prove to them that I was not merely some hot stud with bushy, sexy hair, but that I genuinely deserved to be thought of as a certifiable Hollywood sex criminal!

The Size of My Fingers

The groupie turned out to be someone who talked with food in her mouth. I'm sure that there certainly must (or should) be an officially recognized sexual fetish for talking-with-food-in-the-mouth-as-foreplay. But, my small town upbringing had not given me such inclinations.

With a very full mouth, this woman told me, "I really think you're cute." I could not hear her clearly because her articulation was affected by the food on the roof of her mouth. She could actually have said, "I really like this food," but that's not what I thought that I heard. I instantly imagined what it would feel like if she started spitting food into my face—another apparent sexual fetish known in Los Angeles and other ultra-decadent cities.

Then I noticed that the groupie spent in inordinate amount of time studying my hands. At first, I thought perhaps I unknowingly had cut myself on the way into the restaurant and she could not avert her eyes from my blood because she was a vampire.

She said nothing. I soon remembered I had learned from women about how they like to estimate a man's cock size by examining the size of his fingers.

I desperately wanted to rescue this disastrous encounter as the groupie continued mentally to measure me, as it were. So, I asked her to tell me what kind of music she most enjoyed listening to. I figured that I could not go wrong as a radio guy if I asked her a question about music. This time, the roof of her mouth was completely free of any obstructions when she answered me: "Oh, anything that you play for me on the radio is just fine with me." At that point in the evening, I was crystal clear about the fact that she considered me to be a desirable sex object with large fingers.

Sports can be an aphrodisiac. Even small-town guys know that.

I accepted that all I needed to do was take this woman, as planned, to a Los Angeles Lakers game at the Fabulous Forum and

I would end up being the one who scored. Oh, come on, didn't you expect that sooner or later I would have to throw in at least one sports metaphor?

Somehow, as we sat there together in that deeply romantic venue known as Marie Callender's, I could not clear from my mind the imagery of this woman spitting food from her mouth into my face! That imagery claimed total control of me and succeeded in shutting down all my sexual inclinations—if I even had any such attractions toward women.

That was the precise moment when I decided that I should not take this woman to the Lakers game. Instead, I opted to bid her a fond farewell from the seductive setting of that bakery and pie restaurant parking lot. As I sped away in my VW, I screamed derisive obscenities at myself, first for agreeing to meet her, and secondly for not going any further with her than Santa Monica Boulevard. And, yes, I certainly did check my rearview mirror to make sure that the groupie was not following me.

Years later, after I admitted that I am gay, that whole incident with a female fan in Hollywood stands out as particularly hilarious to me. And, yes, I have looked back and fantasized about what could have happened with me sexually in Hollywood if I had received phone calls from gay men who wanted to be groupies.

Drug Use

Now that I have attempted to cover the not-so-steamy sex part of my story, let me turn to the drug use that I witnessed in Hollywood. The reputation of Hollywood as a decadent den of sin is indelible, if undeserved. After the Drake-Chenault team took over at KIQQ and it became "the new K100," I fully was expecting that genuine rock and roll radio celebrities like Robert W. Morgan and The Real Don Steele would work while openly snorting whatever powders right out in broad daylight. I never saw any of that.

Morgan was on the air in morning drive, and he always was incredibly prepared and focused while he worked on the air on the new K100. Morgan was always just a little too serious and grumpy for my tastes, though. Maybe getting up every day well before sunrise and consuming too many cups of coffee makes a guy become a little more than pissed off at just about everyone. He carefully concealed his typical curmudgeonly way while on the air, however, and always sounded like the friendliest and funniest guy you could ever hope to meet. Morgan was a skilled and talented actor.

Steele, on the other hand, was a true inspiration. No, I never saw him using drugs, either. In my opinion, Steele seemed far too cerebral to need to use any recreational drugs. He seemed to be way, way far above and beyond drugs, if you know what I mean. Steele was a joy to listen to because he always was so clever and quick in his on-air remarks and his comedic timing was perfect. At the radio station when the microphone was switched off, Steele was gracious towards me as if I were somebody important. I'm sure I will never again meet the likes of him.

I will forever remember Steele for giving me the opportunity to attempt to undo the bad karma that I had brought to that Sunset Boulevard radio station. Steele was somehow aware of my editing. Maybe he was so cool and connected that he was somehow plugged into the karmic record, and he just knew I had gutted *Stairway to Heaven*. Maybe the show biz gods from the other dimension who lived inside the walls of the station had told him personally. Maybe Steele, himself, lived in noncorporeal form in that another dimension inside the radio station's walls! I will never know for certain.

One day Steele asked me to produce a stereo remix of *You Can't Sit Down* by the Phil Upchurch Combo. This 1961 recording was used by Steele as the music bed for his signature fractious Friday sign-offs on KHJ. You can experience Steele's KHJ sign-offs today at www.reelradio.com/steele.html. Because KHJ was on the AM dial and AM in those days was not in stereo, Steele had used a mono mix of *You Can't Sit Down* that someone else had edited for him. When Steele arrived to own afternoon drive time on the new K100, naturally he wanted a stereo version of *You Can't Sit Down* because playing music that was not in stereo on an FM radio station just was not cool. Under his direction and guidance in the KIQQ production room, I did physical edits (the old-fashioned way using a razor blade and white splicing tape!) blending both sides of the 45 rpm single into one unique new remix that he subsequently used for his *stereophonic* fractious Friday sign-offs.

Did I see *anyone* using drugs at KIQQ? No, I do not recall having seen anyone using drugs at the station. I certainly knew people in those days who were one-pack-a-day smokers of cigarettes. Drake, Morgan, and, Steele eventually died of cancer that can be traced to their heavy cigarette smoking. But, at KIQQ not only did I never observe anybody smoking marijuana, I never smelled any marijuana smoke in that building the entire time I worked there.

I remember attending some parties hosted by employees from the radio station at their homes. But, even though alcohol consumption was very common and also very visible at those parties, I did not observe anything stereotypical at parties such as wife swapping or hookahs like I naively expected I would find there.

Chapter 6:
Beam Me Up

I was five years old when Walt Disney's second television series, *The Mickey Mouse Club,* premiered on the ABC television network. This captivating daily show for children aired original episodes for four seasons every weekday afternoon, directly targeting my generation, the Baby Boomers. There was just no way to escape being mesmerized by *The Mickey Mouse Club,* with its fresh, young teenage performers such as Annette Funicello, Bobby Burgess, Darlene Gillespie, Tommy Cole, and others, whose names and faces I have remembered my entire life. This unusual television series is known for singing and dancing of talented teenagers. However, I was drawn especially to the serialized dramatic segments featuring teenage actors in *Spin and Marty,* which emphasized cowboy themes, and *The Hardy Boys* with detective mystery themes for young boys.

No surprise that while living within the proverbial white picket fence life of small-town California during the late 1950s, I frequently fantasized about being like one of the guys that I saw every afternoon on *The Mickey Mouse Club.*

A couple of decades later when I came to work in radio in Hollywood, I had matured emotionally past such boyhood fantasies of being an actor on television or in the movies, and I focused instead on having a career in the radio broadcasting industry. Although at KIQQ I worked on the air playing music and announcing using my nickname and surname, Woody Goulart, my main focus as an employee there was not at all an attempt to become a Hollywood radio celebrity or entertainer. I believe that I was born with a decent enough voice that I knew how to use expressively to convey my sense of humor and personality. But, I disliked listening to recordings of my own voice on KIQQ in those days because, to my ears, there are men who have far more appealing announcer voices than mine.

In contrast, I happened to be very skilled at audio production. I developed and produced an ongoing radio documentary series at KIQQ that focused on the business behind the Los Angeles entertainment industries. I named it (deliberately misspelled as) *The K100 Kronicles of Southern California*—a sincere *homage* to the *Pop Chronicles* documentaries broadcast on KRLA that I greatly respected. Unlike those long format productions, however, the unique thing about my work was that my documentary segments were written and produced for airing within the regular music programming and advertising on KIQQ at peak listening times. The more common approach in radio broadcasting in those days was to air documentaries and other public affairs shows in several blocks of programming usually restricted to weekend hours that would not interfere with regular music programming.

I was surprised when my research into the Los Angeles entertainment industries while I worked at KIQQ eventually brought me into the orbits of celebrities. I was allowed access in Burbank to the KNBC television studios where Tom Snyder (1936 - 2007) anchored the 6:00 p.m. newscast before, more famously, going national as the host of NBC's late-night *Tomorrow* program. Interacting with Snyder face-to-face was an exceptional treat for me as a young man who was just starting out in broadcasting.

Snyder came across as so smart and so willing to share his unbridled sense of humor at KNBC. I recorded his voice inside the KNBC studio in which he did a personal endorsement of KIQQ. I even added a music bed of the KNBC news theme to the promo. Of course, as soon as the NBC lawyers heard that promo on KIQQ, the orders quickly came to yank it off the air! During those times when I visited KNBC, I was also able to see, but never interact with, Tom Brokaw and Bryant Gumbel, who both were at the early stages of their careers at NBC in those days.

Roddenberry

For me, the single most memorable "brush with fame" that I experienced while I worked at KIQQ, however, was meeting Gene Roddenberry (1921 - 1991), the creator of *Star Trek*. At that time the NBC television network was launching an animated *Star Trek*, so publicity people from Burbank connected me to Roddenberry so that I might produce a segment that would publicize the new series.

Just four years after the original *Star Trek* starring William Shatner, Leonard Nimoy, and Deforest Kelley had been canceled by NBC, Roddenberry was struggling to keep *Star Trek* alive as either a television or motion picture franchise. What we all know today as "the *Star Trek* phenomenon," that huge and unexpected international popularity of a canceled science fiction television series from the 1960s, had not yet happened. I met Roddenberry before all that. In fact, in 1973 Roddenberry seemed deeply disappointed that his creation had not become a gigantic financial success like he had hoped during the 1960s.

Roddenberry was resistant to talking with me. He admitted over the phone that he very much disliked being interviewed. He told me that he had been "burned" by the media previously. So, I came up with what I thought was a clever idea to use two tape recorders simultaneously while interviewing him at his office in

Burbank. I assured him that if I used those two tape recorders, I could then hand him his own copy of the taped interview before I even left his office so that he would have the original source recordings in the event that I somehow were to edit him to misrepresent his statements.

I was, of course, thrilled when Roddenberry finally agreed to allow me to interview him. Gaining access to someone of his stature was an accomplishment that I could never have dreamed of when I first chose journalism as my major in college. Only small portions of the recordings I made while interviewing Roddenberry were ever broadcast on Los Angeles radio. He was very complimentary of my work, however, and because of him, I subsequently was able to convince other *Star Trek* people to participate in taped interviews—notably writers D.C. Fontana and David Gerrold, and actors DeForest Kelley and Walter Koenig. I also tried to convince Leonard Nimoy and James Doohan to meet me for audio interviews. Nimoy's very-protective assistant kept me away from him completely. I finally got to speak with Doohan on the phone, but he politely declined to be interviewed after I explained that my interviews were a journalistic effort in which the interviewees were not compensated.

From this modest start in the early 1970s as a writer/producer of LA radio documentary segments, my behind-the-scenes journalistic efforts concerning *Star Trek* extended into the future. I remained in contact with Roddenberry over the years because I hoped that I could write a nonfiction book about him and *Star Trek*. I did the next best thing: I went on to write my doctoral dissertation starting in 1977 about the persuasively embedded idea content in the original *Star Trek*. You can read my research findings and conclusions by downloading a pdf of my scholarly work free of charge at my website www.goulartonline.com.

In 1982 when he was on the lecture circuit, I was asked by Roddenberry to introduce him to a large crowd in New Haven, Connecticut. Afterwards, he invited me to dine with him at a local New Haven steakhouse—an experience I will never forget.

What I proved to myself by writing and producing the *Star Trek* radio documentary segments was astonishing to me. I was just a small-town kid, who was somehow driven by an insatiable curiosity and an adventurous spirit. I learned a very valuable life lesson when I was only in my twenties: **What you can imagine in your mind, you can make real in your life.** This Old Testament philosophy about the crucial importance of what you hold true in your heart and mind turned out to be genuine and not just some ancient writings from long-dead zealots.

So it was that I became completely convinced while working at KIQQ that it is totally valid and sensible—as The Real Don Steele consistently taught his listeners—to find a quest for adventure in your life. That has motivated me continually throughout my life into the present.

Chapter 7:
Tracing the Timeline

Let me trace the timeline of KHJ radio for you to provide a way for you to understand why people still remember this radio station half a century after Boss Radio KHJ:

When it started broadcasting on April 13, 1922, KHJ became the second radio station on the air in Los Angeles. Known as "The Times Radiophone" because of being owned by the *Los Angeles Times* newspaper, the station was housed within a 10-foot by 12-foot room atop the original LA Times building. The famous transmitter site where the radio towers for KHJ were located the Fairfax district of Los Angeles is now gone. But, you still can drive or walk by the building at 5515 Melrose Avenue in Hollywood where the studios of KHJ in 1960s were located.

Back in those early days, newspapers regarded radio as competition. If you were a newspaper company that could own a radio station, well then, that would be a whole different matter! Since KHJ was owned by a powerful Los Angeles newspaper company, the station derived benefits from the corporation's considerable promotional reach. Most notably, the affiliation with the *Los Angeles Times* pumped up the resale value of KHJ. Don

Lee, a successful Cadillac dealer in Southern California, bought the station from the newspaper, and ultimately KHJ and the entire network (operated by Lee's son Thomas after his father died) was merged into RKO Radio.

As I already mentioned, those famous call letters were intended to convey a sense of "Kindness, Happiness and Joy." You would not believe that at one time, the early KHJ signed-off each night with an announcer reciting this poem:

> May kindness, happiness and joy
> be with you all the day.
> And may the God who loves us all
> Forget not KHJ!
>
> God will not fail to watch thy sleep
> And wake thee with his light.
> And now dear friends of KHJ
> I wish you all goodnight.

In these gloriously politically correct days of the 21st century, can you imagine a station signing off with a poem like that? And unlike today when stations broadcast 24 hours a day, in the earliest days of radio, KHJ and all stations of the day, had to sign off for three minutes out of every 15 so that any potential distress calls might be heard from ships at sea.

I can just imagine the announcer opening his microphone to say, "Okay, Los Angeles, we'll be right back to the big band sound after we take a short time-out for distress calls from all the guys slogging away on those fishing boats off Santa Catalina."

Another major difference in those days before the invention of tape recorders was that radio, out of necessity, had to rely upon live (not recorded) broadcasts. It was possible to make one-of-a-kind recordings on phonograph disks of actual radio broadcasts. But until audiotape was invented in Germany in 1928, recorded radio broadcasts were cumbersome and suffered from pops and cracks inherent to phonograph recordings of that era.

That was Then; This is Now

In the 1960s, KHJ, which had been located at different frequencies since the 1920s, ended up at 930 on the AM dial. Popular music of the day on AM radio was the prevailing standard in the broadcasting business back then. It wasn't until the 1970s that FM radio emerged as the standard for music broadcasting. AM radio today is known especially for broadcasting the talk radio format, such as on at KFI, Los Angeles—one of the oldest stations in that market.

Popular music hits—once exclusively intended for people's ears—morphed into multimedia products with video along with the audio thanks to major changes in technology. In 1981, Music

Television MTV became the first channel to show music videos exclusively. Popular music is almost always emphasizes the visual element today because of YouTube and other online video channels. Young people today can choose not to listen to radio at all. This is possible because popular music hits are available on demand with videos on television and on iTunes as well as on Pandora.

The passive experience of listening to a radio station that controls when particular songs are played can be perceived as the exact opposite of the active experience of instant, on-demand playback of specific songs using hand-held or computerized devices. Radio programming as it has been known for so many decades will need to change with the times and the technology. If the business of radio programming is to remain relevant in the years to come, someone will need to figure out some other way to engage and maintain a sufficiently large audience. What happened in San Francisco in 2011 at radio station KGO—a format change resulting in job losses for many older employees—can be expected to happen again in other markets. This is because younger audience members have already started abandoning radio broadcasting and have switched to hand-held or computerized devices as their primary source to participate in pop culture.

This cultural shift that we are seeing happening during the second decade of the 21st century is precisely why I feel it is vital for us all to remember the 20th century when radio stations attracted significant audiences of the exact demographic groups so desirable to advertisers. Those days were, indeed, glorious because of the people who appeared on the air. KHJ in the early days employed many famous entertainers whose careers began at the station. Eddie Cantor, and, George Burns and Gracie Allen—all famous names from a bygone era—are notable examples. Pat Weaver (the celebrated president of the National Broadcasting Company and father of actor Sigourney Weaver) was an announcer at KHJ in 1934.

During the big band era, KHJ had its own 50-piece orchestra. In 1931, crooner Bing Crosby made nightly trips to KHJ where he sang over the air for 15 minutes six nights per week. In the mid-1940's, comic genius Steve Allen led the morning team with his show called, "Smile Time." Allen returned to KHJ in the 1960s as host of a regularly scheduled live remote broadcast with his wife, Jayne Meadows, from their home in the San Fernando Valley.

On April 12, 1945, Franklin Delano Roosevelt died after serving as president since 1933. No other person was President of the United States longer than FDR. The 22nd Amendment in 1951 set term limits so no other person will ever again attain this distinction. Not yet even 10 years of age, Philip Yarbrough (who would become known in adulthood as Bill Drake) witnessed the emotional impact of the radio announcement of FDR's death and made the connection in his mind that radio could be used in powerful ways to affect people.

RKO Adventures

By the 1960s, live programming featuring celebrities on the radio was starting to be considered old fashioned and out of vogue in Los Angeles, especially in comparison to the rock and roll radio programming available on other LA stations such as KFWB and KRLA. Those in charge of RKO General knew that unless the programming on their Los Angeles station KHJ was updated to a sound or format that was more appealing to large numbers of people, KHJ's financial performance would never improve.

Arguably, the RKO production output, reputation, identity, and brand all were essential to the very history of Hollywood, itself. To understand how corporations such as RKO owned and controlled entertainment properties like KHJ radio requires spending a little time exploring a complex set of purchases and sales that altered the very landscape of the entertainment business over the decades. Many very famous people and companies at one time or another have become part of the overall RKO story.

In 1925, Joseph P. Kennedy (the father of President John Fitzgerald Kennedy) purchased Film Booking Office (FBO)

Studios in Hollywood. The elder Kennedy, who had a deep appreciation for the financial viability of motion picture entertainment, bought into other film companies so that FBO Studios ultimately included companies named Keith, Orpheum, and Pathé. Keith is the "K" and Orpheum is the "O" in RKO. Then, David Sarnoff, the founder and president of the Radio Corporation of America (RCA), the parent company of the National Broadcasting Company (NBC), pooled his financial resources with Kennedy's film interests, adding the "R." The resulting merger created a company named RKO Radio Pictures.

The strongly positive reputation of RKO Radio Pictures was solidified with such classic films as the original *King Kong* in 1933, numerous Fred Astaire and Ginger Rogers musicals, and most importantly, *Citizen Kane* by Orson Welles in 1941, which is often cited as the best American film of all time. Billionaire aviator Howard Hughes bought controlling interest of RKO in 1948, but he then nearly destroyed the company with his eccentric approaches to the filmmaking business.

Desilu Productions, a television and movie company known for *I Love Lucy, Star Trek, and Mission Impossible,* was founded by the pioneering husband-and-wife television duo, Desi Arnaz and Lucille Ball. Desilu purchased the RKO studio lot in Hollywood on Melrose Avenue in 1957, and later sold it to Paramount Pictures.

The motion picture side of the original RKO continued to exist in various corporate forms until 1989 when Dina Merrill and Ted Hartley purchased RKO Pictures. The unique legacy is that RKO is that it became the oldest of the continuously operating movie studios.

The Self-Destruction of RKO Radio

The broadcasting side of RKO developed on both the east and west coasts of the United States and subsequently suffered a self-inflicted demise. In 1943, the General Tire and Rubber Company entered broadcasting with its purchase of The Yankee Network, Incorporated and its stations, including WNAC-AM/FM/TV in Boston. The stations continued to operate under the Yankee Network banner. Then in 1950, General Tire and Rubber purchased Thomas S. Lee Enterprises Incorporated, doing business as The Don Lee Network, Incorporated named after its founder, Cadillac dealer Don Lee (father of Thomas S. Lee), whose primary stations were KHJ-AM/FM/TV in Los Angeles.

In 1952, General Tire and Rubber purchased Bamberger Broadcasting Company, owner of WOR-AM/FM/TV in New York City and merged the stations into The Don Lee Network. After purchasing the former RKO Radio Pictures from Howard Hughes (minus the motion picture lot that went to Desilu), all of the stations that General Tire owned were merged into General Teleradio Incorporated. Two beneficiaries of the RKO motion picture library were channel 9 in New York, WOR-TV, and channel 9 in Los Angeles, KHJ-TV. General Tire merged its broadcasting and film operations into RKO Teleradio Pictures Incorporated, and ultimately changed the company name to RKO General Incorporated.

Most people may know that in the United States, over-the-air broadcasting is federally regulated by the Federal Communications Commission (FCC). There is insufficient space here to cover the complete history of how the FCC came to be. What I think is very important to understand, however, is the reason why there is federal regulation today: Regulating the assignments and usage of over-the-air broadcasting frequencies in the United States emerged as a crucial need when the first radio stations were started by various different, competing companies. Imagine the chaos that would have occurred in those days if all were free to choose any over-the-air broadcasting frequency at will.

I have stated clearly elsewhere in this book that I believe that no federal agency should be funded with taxpayer dollars to regulate programming content, advertising sales, and other such elements. Technical issues such a frequency usage or effective radiated power of the transmitters could be managed by private industry. There is an everyday reality that the FCC as we know it in the present day is inescapably stuck in a partisan political environment: When a Republican gets elected to the office of President of the United States, a Republican can be expected to be appointed to be the Commissioner of the FCC. When there is a Democrat in the White House, the normal expectation is for a Democrat to get appointed as FCC Commissioner.

This is not a unique characteristic of the FCC. Federal appointments (known affectionately inside the Washington, DC Beltway as "plum jobs") are found throughout the United States government, and not just in the Washington, DC area. You have to decide for yourself whether the established system of political appointments to federal positions produces the best possible choices in people to run the government. My views on this should be crystal clear, however.

RKO descended into infamy in the history of American radio and television companies because the company became entangled with the FCC over non-technical regulatory issues. Starting in the 1980s, stemming from allegations that RKO General violated federal laws, the FCC forced the corporation to relinquish all of its radio and television broadcasting licenses and sell the station facilities to new licensees at equipment value only.

Many people who worked at RKO in the radio and television business remain very proud of their work to the present day. But, the license revocations by the FCC in several large markets tore the broadcasting side of the company apart and left what I consider to be a permanent scar upon the radio and television broadcasting industry.

To understand what happened, it is best to start by looking back on what RKO owned before their legal problems with the federal government. Then it is possible to understand the sheer magnitude of the losses RKO suffered: WNAC-TV channel 7 in Boston was the first station license of RKO General to be revoked. Channel 7 in Boston became WNEV-TV owned by New England Television on May 1, 1982. You may wonder what happened to the parent corporation, General Tire and Rubber Company. In 1984, the company reappeared as GenCorp, a major technology-based manufacturing company headquartered in Sacramento, California.

The cascading impact of the destruction of RKO radio and television stations crashed through other major markets like a tsunami. The company was bought by United Stations, later known as Unistar. Corporate mergers followed and RKO/Unistar was bought by Infinity, ultimately part of CBS Radio, which, in turn, was bought by Viacom. RKO General's KHJ-TV channel 9 in Los Angeles was the last station license to be pulled. Channel 9 in Los

Angeles became KCAL-TV in 1990 owned by the Walt Disney Company. Disney bought Capital Cities/ABC in 1995. Less than 40 years after *Disneyland* had debuted as one Sunday night show on ABC, the Walt Disney Company had come to own the entire television network. Disney later sold KCAL-TV to Young Broadcasting and then in 2002, CBS Corporation bought the station.

In short, it was people at RKO who brought this destruction of a company's brand and financial viability upon themselves. There simply is no one else to credit or blame but **certain people employed at RKO who did shitty jobs of protecting the huge financial value of a once-great corporation**. Blaming the FCC or the courts for the demise of the RKO radio operations is a complete deflection of responsibility away from individuals who mismanaged RKO radio into financial ruin. Hopefully, other employees representing other broadcasting companies will learn about RKO Radio and learn not to make the same (or similar) mistakes.

In the present day, it is very easy to find examples of one corporation owning and operating more than one radio and television station in the same market. This routine way of doing business today literally was against federal law in the past. I happen to share the belief that today's routine multiple media outlet ownership in individual markets greatly diminished what was once a wider diversity of content choices available to audience members. But, I accept the reality that your average citizen does not care about diversity of content choices.

Chapter 8:
Uncovering and Preserving Radio Programming History

It turns out that I was not destined to have a long career in LA radio. My employment did not end because of technology, however. The end for me arrived in 1974 when Bill Watson, who headed day-to-day programming and production at KIQQ under Bill Drake and Gene Chenault, said some variation of those famous words for which Donald Trump would later become famous: "You're fired!"

I was treated with courtesy and respect in my termination, even though, to the Drake-Chenault people, I definitely was "an outsider." Gene Chenault personally made sure that I got severance pay equaling two full weeks of work. And nobody said an unkind word to me at any point in my transition out. I report all this here to dispel a prevailing myth that the Drake-Chenault people were ruthless and heavy-handed. I never saw any of that when I worked at KIQQ.

Steve Jobs wrote that getting fired from Apple turned out to be a hugely positive experience for him. Not right away, but eventually. I feel that my getting fired from KIQQ taught me similar lessons, but unfortunately for me, I never have enjoyed wealth like Steve Jobs had during his short life.

After I became unemployed in Los Angeles, during early 1974 I started to reevaluate my goals in my personal and professional life. While I searched for work in Southern California, I also wanted to be realistic and look beyond the immediate horizon of what was familiar and comfortable for me.

I entered a time of intense self-examination about what I was doing with my life. I felt depressed that I could not find full-time replacement work in the radio broadcasting business in Southern California. Those were the days of long lines at gas stations because there was a so-called "national energy crisis" going on. The once plentiful supply of petroleum products had become severely limited within our country for a variety of reasons. In turn, the US economy experienced *stagflation*—high inflation of prices with accompanying stagnated economic growth. This meant that the local economy in Southern California at that time was not at all conducive to finding employment.

Looking back over my life, it seems to me that there is always one crisis or another that sours the US economy. In the 1970s, I felt deeply heartbroken that I no longer worked for the Drake-Chenault team in Hollywood. I had fantasized for years about living and working in Los Angeles. Now what was I going to do? My fantasy came true for a very short while. But, what does a guy do when his fantasy is over? Go back and start a new life in the same old small town?

I was very immature emotionally at that time when I was only 23. Yet, I somehow attained a clear understanding about my need right away to make a very smart choice about my professional life. Remaining in Los Angeles seemed at that time to be an incredibly foolish potential choice for me. The negatives outweighed the positives. For instance, it was normal in those days to wait for up to a full 60 minutes throughout the Los Angeles area just to fill up your car's tank with gas. For me, being a participant in long lines at gas stations with hundreds of my fellow Los Angeles residents was the trigger event in my life that motivated me to relocate somewhere else with a lower population and fewer vehicles.

I was the product of the "learn by doing" education system at Cal Poly University in San Luis Obispo. I had earned a Bachelor of Science degree in journalism. I had worked professionally in radio broadcasting in the number two media market in the United States. Now I was unemployed. If wondered if my B.S. degree stood for Bull Shit.

The personal economic reality of my job loss in Hollywood rock and roll radio forced me to consider that my undergraduate degree in journalism was not enough to save me in and of itself. Rather suddenly, I lost all idealism and innocent naïveté about the value of having an undergraduate degree in journalism especially during a tough economy.

Escape from Los Angeles

I needed something more for myself. The year 2011 would become a benchmark. One of the academic majors with the highest level of unemployment that year was journalism. Back in 1974, I experienced a sneak preview of what can happen to a person who seeks to pursue a tightly focused career in the journalism profession. I reasoned that my unemployment was but a temporary issue. But, in my heart, I believed that I needed to look for career choices outside of the relatively narrow field of journalism. It was time to redefine who I was and, if necessary, reinvent and rebrand myself in some completely different direction starting by getting out of LA.

I was reeling from the emotional pain of not being able to remain employed in Hollywood rock and roll radio. I felt that I had succeeded in broadcast journalism. I had proven that to myself by writing and producing the Los Angeles radio documentaries at

KIQQ in which I told interesting stories about topics of interest to Southern California. Yet, I also realized that I could only increase my potential to make a living if I broadened what I was prepared to do professionally beyond the narrow field of journalism.

This powerful personal insight about the need for me to stop limiting myself to journalism careers provided me with a realistic, yet sobering, perspective on the loss of my Hollywood rock and roll radio job. I believed that I was sufficiently intelligent and talented that I could learn new skills beyond journalism towards whatever my next career might be. So, that was the direction I took. This was the first instance in my life of what I now consider to be an ongoing process of reinvention and rebranding of myself.

My first choice was to remain at a California university since I did not want to leave my home state. As a California resident, I had a "local" status. Compared to going to some out of state university, I knew that if I remained in the state of California, I could certainly get a high-quality graduate school education at a reasonable price.

As much as I loved Los Angeles for the fun that I could find there, I came to realize that I needed to grow up as a man and start to focus on more important things in life than merely seeking to have fun. So, I chose to go to graduate school at Humboldt State University located in the very small town of Arcata, California.

I knew of that remote location because my parents had taken me and my siblings on a Humboldt County "fishing vacation" when I was in my early teenage years. A "fishing vacation" in this specific context was a multigenerational family vacation in Trinidad, California during which my father's father, Tony Goulart, and my father's mother, Katherine Goulart, were present. In the morning, my grandfather and my father and his brother, Lawrence Goulart, would go fishing in the hopes of catching salmon.

Then, later in the day, after the men had returned with the salmon, it was time for the women to take over. My grandmother and my mother and my aunt, Mary Goulart, would clean the salmon, cut it up, and then put the fish parts into cans. A clear hierarchy was in effect. The men had their work. The women had theirs.

Since I was just a kid and never was allowed to go out fishing for salmon, I had no way to know what the men's work was like. But, I saw with my own eyes that the women's work there in Trinidad, California was very messy and, yes, smelly work. Sounds very old-school, doesn't it? Yes, it certainly was.

The whole purpose of the Trinidad "fishing vacation" was to produce an inventory of canned salmon that the extended Goulart family could eat during the months ahead. Once I reached adulthood, I discovered that salmon, if cooked properly like a steak, can taste wonderful. But, in those days when I was just a kid, I never liked the fishy taste of salmon that was canned by the women of my family in Trinidad, California.

We all camped out on that "fishing vacation" in not-very-fancy vacation trailers that each had to be towed over 500 miles from where we lived on the Central California coast. The whole "fishing vacation" emphasized "back-to-nature" aspects of staying for several days and nights within a public campground near the Pacific Ocean. I do not remember feeling deprived in terms of the comforts of sleeping inside our family's vacation trailer. But, I do recall using a not-very-fancy sleeping bag.

One very positive memory I retained from this "fishing vacationing" at Trinidad, California was the amazing redwood trees. Those famously tall redwood trees where what "sold" me on the idea I had to relocate from Los Angeles to Humboldt County.

There is one other factor, of course, why I wanted to be in that area filled with redwood trees. If you look at a Google map, you will discover that Humboldt County is roughly 700 miles north of Los Angeles when driving northward through my hometown of San Luis Obispo. I told myself that if I lived 700 miles away from Los Angeles, the great distance certainly would help me focus on what I was going to do next in my career without maintaining any connections back to my old life in Southern California.

Leaving Radio Behind

I was accepted into the master's degree program in communication at Humboldt State University in 1974 thanks, in part, to a strong referral from Cal Poly journalism professor Ed Zuchelli. Communication sounded to me like it would provide me with a sufficiently broader field of study compared to journalism. That was a big plus. Yet, once I relocated to the Eureka area, I discovered that the local economy was equally bad, if not worse, than the economy in Los Angeles. That was a big minus. The area had one significant positive trait, however. I was happy to discover that there were no long lines at gas stations in the Eureka area like I had experienced in Los Angeles.

As a California resident, I qualified for lower education fees compared to what out-of-state students had to pay. Then, I was offered the opportunity to teach undergraduate courses while working on my master's degree. Do so qualified me to receive an educational stipend to help me pay for my living expenses. I had never considered making a living as a university instructor. How strange and sudden a career change this was for me compared to working very recently in Hollywood rock and roll radio!

Once I found success in teaching university courses at Humboldt State University, I began to consider that getting out of the radio broadcasting profession was a wise choice for me. I started to envision myself in a full-time career as a university professor rather than seeking to return to radio. Several of my friends who remained working in the radio business at that time urged me not to "leave radio behind."

Going Back into the Neon Fun Jungle

When the time arrived for me to select a subject of study for my master's thesis at Humboldt State University, I chose to examine Los Angeles rock and roll radio during the 1960s. I will always carry a part of Los Angeles in my heart and soul no matter where I may choose to go. I felt a strong attraction to rock and roll radio programming as the subject of my research, so I went with the strength of my feelings. More specifically, my choice was to study the work of the Drake-Chenault radio programming team starting at KHJ in Los Angeles in 1965.

Incredibly, even though I had proposed to study rock and roll radio—not a conservative choice for someone in a graduate-level academic program—I received all the required academic permissions to proceed. My advisor, communication professor James E. Seward, was a steadfast inspiration to me. He urged me to take this difficult project as far as I could.

I soon discovered that I had to go out and conduct primary research. This particular method was necessary because learning about this subject of rock and roll radio in Hollywood was not something that one could accomplish by going to the library and checking out some books. When I began my research in 1975 there were few book-length sources for historical and cultural information about any contemporary United States radio programming, let alone books about the accomplishments of Bill Drake and Gene Chenault in programming rock and roll radio stations.

I came to realize that I had chosen an incredibly difficult subject matter. The main obstacle was that in order to have my efforts qualify as primary research, I needed to conduct in-person interviews with eyewitnesses and participants. Everybody that I needed to interview face-to-face lived hundreds of miles away from where I lived in Eureka, California. Now what?

I never stopped to consider what might happen if anybody simply declined my requests for in-person interviews. Failure was just never an option for me. I just went out into the real world, very strongly believing in myself and my ability to convince eyewitnesses and participants to sit down and talk with me face to face about rock and roll radio programming. Of course, that meant I had to return for more adventures in the neon fun jungle.

The Indignities of Small-Market Radio

At heart, I am an essentially modest man. Not once did I look at myself as having felt like I was on some mission to become some important historian of contemporary American radio programming or whatever. The very most that I wanted to accomplish in those days was an honest perspective into the individual worlds of eyewitnesses and participants in rock and roll radio programming in Los Angeles.

I wanted to succeed as a credible writer of nonfiction, but in all honesty, thoughts of achieving acclaim or financial reward for my efforts never crossed my mind. I also believed that because I had felt passion about the radio broadcasting industry, I would be someone who could write about that industry with credibility.

To augment my academic stipend that I earned from part-time teaching of undergraduate communications courses at Humboldt State University, I found part-time radio production and announcing work in the Eureka media market. I worked at KFMI, an FM station licensed to Eureka, and also at KNCR, which stood for "North Coast Radio," a daytime-only AM station licensed to Fortuna. Holding two part-time jobs at the same time while also being a full-time graduate student was very challenging for me. I did not sleep as many hours at night as I should have. Nor did I invest any efforts into getting into a relationship with anyone. So, I grew to feel very lonely when I lived in Humboldt County. But, the experiences I had while there helped me to grow up and stop looking at life as merely an opportunity to seek pleasure.

It certainly was not at all fun to work in Eureka radio especially after I had just come from working in Los Angeles radio. I quickly discovered that the level of professionalism and attention to detail in Eureka radio were significantly lower than what were the standards in Los Angeles. Anyone who attempts to make such a jump from very large media market way down to a very small media market invites the exact kind of culture shock that I experienced in Eureka. I would not wish that on anybody. As I struggled to remain sane in Eureka radio while working with unprofessional colleagues who had no major market experience, the thought of becoming a full-time university professor as a career alternative became an obsession for me.

Weed

I write elsewhere in this book that while I worked in Southern California in the 1970s, I did not come into contact with people who smoked marijuana. In stunning contrast, I discovered that Northern California at that time was the main place in California that attracted people who wanted to smoke marijuana. Rent the 2008 motion picture named *Humboldt County* and you can receive a very inexpensive and totally entertaining 90-minute education about marijuana usage in that colorful Northern California region.

You may think that I am being sarcastic or cruel, but I'm really only attempting to be honest about marijuana usage. For many people, smoking a joint in Humboldt County in the 1970s was considered routine and ordinary like consuming a bottle of beer. My introduction to marijuana came by way of a fellow graduate student. He baked "special" brownies for a party that I attended in Eureka. But, he deliberately chose not to tell me about the secret ingredient until I had finished off three or four of those delicious chocolate wonders!

For me, as a young man at age 25, having this brand new experience of eating weed in a dessert was simultaneously horrifying and mind-blowing. Right now, if you were watching a documentary instead of reading a book, this would be the point in the storytelling where you start to hear sitar music in the background and see psychedelic neon images flashed across your screen. If you close your eyes and imagine, you may just hear the music of Ravi Shankar.

While you're imagining that you hear Indian music, let me move on to the science part of our show: Human lungs can process the effects of marijuana much faster than intestines ever can. This explains why people who want a quick high will make the choice to smoke weed instead of eating it!

Somehow, I was smart enough to avoid falling into the daily routine use of marijuana in Humboldt County like I saw so many other young people around me were doing. Instead, I focused on my studies. Looking back on those days, I'm sure there are many who knew me who were far more laid back and experimental than me. I know that I came across as more than just a little old-fashioned and stuffy compared to them because I was not interested in getting high every day by smoking pot. More importantly, when I shared my fantasies with some of my friends in Eureka about using my research into Hollywood rock and roll radio as the way I was going to free myself from what I perceived as the limitations of living in Humboldt County, they literally laughed at me.

I kept my focus on completing graduate school and escaping from Humboldt County, which I did not think was a healthy place for me to remain. I envisioned redefining and rebranding myself as a full-time university professor somewhere else. My professional goal in those days was to have the financial means from teaching college to be a nonfiction writer. I was really ignorant about the reality that people in those days did not make much money teaching college!

Beyond Humboldt

After Humboldt, I went on to complete my doctorate in communications at Indiana University. I did not think of myself then as an overachiever back then, but the reality is I earned three university degrees before I had even reached the age of 30. My first job as a full-time university professor started in 1979 in Louisville, Kentucky. Then, from 1980 through 1982, I taught full-university courses in the New Haven, Connecticut area.

The low pay in academia eventually motivated me to once again redefine and rebrand myself. I did exactly that by switching to a new career path in which I left academia to work instead in various management positions in the cable television industry in Massachusetts and Arizona for a decade. I later worked for nearly two decades in the Washington, DC market in strategic

communications leadership positions for the American Association
of Retired Persons (AARP) and later as a consultant for the
Defense Department, the Justice Department, and the United States
Army. I continued my communications consultancy in Las Vegas,
Nevada for over a year before relocating back to my home state to
work in San Francisco in digital marketing for an international
bank for another year or so before ultimately relocating back again
to Las Vegas.

Chasing Down Interviewees

While I buckled down and focused on my research into Boss
Radio in the 1970s, I was aware of the pressure I was placing upon
myself to do a credible job. I set my sights upon uncovering and
reporting what I discovered through my primary research efforts. I
invested in myself. I spent what little money I had during graduate
school at Humboldt State University to travel by air from Eureka
to San Francisco to interview radio columnist Bill Gavin. That
proved to be an excellent place for me to start. Gavin was a crucial
advisor to me in selecting the correct people to interview. But, I
also relied upon those whom I interviewed to suggest other people.
This networking prevented me from veering off into irrelevant
sources.

I traveled to Los Angeles to interview Bill Drake, Gene Chenault, *Billboard* columnist Claude Hall and others who were either participants or eyewitnesses to what Drake and Chenault had accomplished. On one visit to my hometown of San Luis Obispo, I also drove to Fresno (over two and half hours one-way) to interview Ken Devaney, who was general manager at KHJ when Boss Radio was launched in 1965.

The longest journey I made for my face-to-face interviews was to and from Eureka to San Diego by air. That interview proved to be a major turning point in my life. I spent several hours at the LaJolla home of Ron Jacobs talking with him while my cassette tape machine captured all that we said. I regret that I do not still have those tapes!

My Research Findings and Conclusions

Once I had gathered all the interview tapes together and personally transcribed them, I finished what I had started. I successfully completed original, primary research built upon face-to-face interviews with eyewitnesses and participants in the radio programming business who had never before—or since—been interviewed together for one publication. I incorporated information and quotations from the interviews and other primary source materials into my master's thesis that was published at

Humboldt State University in fulfillment of the legal requirements for earning my master's degree in communication in 1976.

My primary research gave me evidence to help me conclude that what caused the business failure of the Drake-Chenault team in the radio industry was *groupthink*. I became aware of this fascinating term from a 1972 book, *Victims of groupthink; a psychological study of foreign-policy decisions and fiascoes* by Irving Janis. That pioneering research by Janis described a real-world phenomenon that can start organically and grow out of control within a closely-knit group of people. The affected group highly and passionately values and defends conformity that promotes an irreversible fall into dysfunctional behaviors leading directly to bad decisions.

All the creativity and innovativeness of the Drake-Chenault team was insufficient to stop the spread of groupthink, which ultimately in the 1970s eroded the business success of the team. Here is a summary of the major findings from my primary research:

- Several radio broadcasting professionals, independent of each other, all are in agreement about the fact that Bill Drake should not have been credited by the radio industry trade press as the person most responsible for the success of Boss Radio.

- Bill Drake and Gene Chenault angered and alienated several of their key management people working on Boss Radio by taking radio programming components that were tested and perfected by Boss Radio and using those components to program radio stations in San Francisco, Boston, and other major markets.

- The failure of Bill Drake and Gene Chenault to hold together a successful team while programming the RKO Radio chain of rock and roll radio stations was caused by the deterioration of mental efficiency, the lack of proper reality testing, and the suppression of dissenting viewpoints—symptoms which are critically destructive to successful group behavior and decision-making—today commonly referred to as groupthink.

- After being ousted from RKO Radio, Bill Drake and Gene Chenault unsuccessfully attempted to recapture their national prominence as successful radio programmers at a Los Angeles FM station called "K100." That venture failed financially in the late 1970s.

If you are interested in learning more, please visit www.bossradioforever.com where you can download a free pdf of my original research. Also, you may want to search on Google using the phrase "Boss Radio Woody Goulart" to see all related information currently available online that is associated together with that subject and my name.

All my work researching and reporting on the accomplishments of talented professionals in the radio broadcasting industry probably would have been completely forgotten were it not for the internet. *I believe that one of the very worst things that can happen to anyone is to be forgotten.*

Online Efforts

It is very common for people who write a master's thesis or a doctoral dissertation for graduate degrees to later publish their work in other forms to share their findings with a wider audience. That's exactly what I did. I finally reached my professional goal of being a nonfiction writer.

In 1996, I launched a radio history website about Boss Radio that I initially named the Boss Radio Information Site. How bland can you get with a website name? I later revised the site and rebranded it as Boss Radio Forever. Due to being hacked and having content ruined online, I had to take steps to preserve my work better. The intellectual property comprised of my research (interviews, letters and so forth) plus the conclusions I drew remain under my ownership and control. This book contains content that I adapted from my original research dating back to the 1970s along with additional research that I conducted well into the 21st century.

My use of the internet starting in the late 1990s to share my research and commentary about rock and roll radio programming turned out to be yet another instance in my life where I have chosen to reinvent and rebrand myself. I did not intend to make waves or bring attention to myself by using the internet to publish my research findings and conclusions about Boss Radio KHJ from my late 1970s efforts at Humboldt State University. Modestly, I presumed that it was only natural for a writer to use the internet to share his writing with a wider audience that was possible using other channels of communication.

Chapter 9:
Adventures with Ron Jacobs

I did not know that my choice to use the internet in the late 1990s would change my life. Here's what happened: In 1996, a newspaper in Santa Ana, California (the *Orange County Register*) published comments from Ron Jacobs about my online writing on the subject of Boss Radio KHJ. Jacobs was the original KHJ program director 1965 to 1969 who implemented the Boss Radio format. Without him, the format might never have been as successful as it was.

Jacobs returned to his native Hawaii after several years in Southern California. The one and only time that Jacobs and I ever met face-to-face was in 1975 when I visited him in LaJolla, California where I interviewed him about Boss Radio KHJ. Then, unexpectedly, one day in 1996, I received an email from Gary Lycan (1944 – 2013), the well-known radio columnist at a newspaper in Southern California. Lycan wanted to give me the opportunity to respond to criticism from Jacobs that had been printed in the *Orange County Register*.

Back in the 1990s, I had wondered what it would feel like if I fell into obscurity. I finished my primary research on Boss Radio KHJ, wrote my thesis, and received my master's degree. Then I went on to earn a doctoral degree. I wrote my Ph.D. dissertation about *Star Trek* and other science fiction television programming. And I imagined that would be that.

But, then the internet came along. I chose to adapt my content about Boss Radio KHJ and publish an online version. I truly was modest and honestly about expecting absolutely nothing at all to come of my online writing about Boss Radio KHJ.

But, quite the opposite happened. What got published in the *Orange County Register* about me and my work changed my perceptions about myself, which in turn changed my future.

Ron Jacobs was quoted in the newspaper expressing his opinion that I had no credibility because I was not present at KHJ in Los Angeles when Boss Radio happened. Here are his exact words published in Santa Ana, California on September 1, 1996:

I wrote him [Woody Goulart] that he had no right to print material from an interview granted from a 26-year-old discussion intended only for an academic paper, that his "report" was superficial, and that he had no direct knowledge of what happened at KHJ during the important years (in my

opinion, from 1965-1070; I was there from the start in May 1965 through mid-1969), and his work with Drake in later years did not qualify him in any way as knowledgeable about the subject of KHJ. It's nice that someone remembers KHJ, however, incorrect and revisionist facts serve no purpose.

Jacobs stated that he thought my work was of little value because it was intended merely as a "school report" and implied that nobody values scholarship. He clearly was attempting to be as insulting as possible by his choice of such a phrase as if to dismissively say with as much cruelty as humanly possible, *"Oh look, little nobody Woody wrote a silly 'book report' and it means nothing at all to anyone of importance."*

That *Orange County Register* coverage of little nobody Woody and his silly "book report" attracted more attention than I ever could have accomplished on my own. I was ready to tell Ron Jacobs to fuck off. But, I didn't. This is because I realized I should take advantage of the situation to attract additional readers—the exact opposite of what Jacobs wanted.

I revised my site after the *Orange County Register* incident to present myself in the best possible light if/when others came to look. I presumed that I would never again hear from Ron Jacobs. But, I was wrong. After I had posted my website revisions online, I received this email from Jacobs:

Date: Sun, 16 Feb 1997 21:59:18 -0800
From: Ronald Jacobs <whodaguy@earthlink.net>
To: wg@smart.net
Subject: New site format

Just saw your revised site and it is indeed an improvement.
There are still a bunch of quibbles I have about details, but then
again, I'm an anal-retentive Virgo who only remembers the old
stuff when asked. I wish we could do an update interview.

The direct outcome of that email Jacobs sent to me was my
decision to work with him collaboratively rather than merely
continuing to piss him off from afar. For several years on and off
until his death in 2016, Jacobs provided anecdotes and
commentaries for me in lengthy emails and over the phone in
extended phone calls about Boss Radio KHJ that I could share
online with his permission.

Either he was merely crazy and wildly unpredictable, or, I had
"proven something" to Jacobs by surviving his heated criticisms
and lengthy suggestions as I rewrote my online coverage of the
history of Boss Radio KHJ. Although I really did not care about
gaining the approval of Jacobs, or anyone else, I was pleased that,
together with Jacobs, I crafted what is an accurate historical
perspective on Boss Radio KHJ in the neon fun jungle.

My online writing about Boss Radio KHJ demonstrated what's
possible to accomplish using what was back then called "new

media" technology beyond print and broadcast media. I believe that I inspired Jacobs to use this "new" technology that he otherwise might never have considered using. He eventually did get his own website during the late 1990s and ultimately wrote the book, quite literally, about Boss Radio KHJ. It was published first in paperback form in 2000, but I provided the essential editorial leadership so Jacobs could get an eBook version of *KHJ Inside Boss Radio* published a dozen years later for Amazon Kindle devices.

For his eBook, Jacobs relied upon the assistance of Carol Williams (the wife of one of the original 93/KHJ Boss Jocks, Johnny Williams) as his editor. She provided years of editorial assistance to him to upgrade the paperback book into what would become the eBook version in 2012. My participation proved to bring this over the finished line following many technical problems with the eBook that he and Carol Williams just could not resolve on their own.

I also had hands-on responsibility for producing the Hawaii-themed website for Ron Jacobs that he named "Whodaguy Hawaii" after on an on-air nickname he had. My investment of energy, time, and, yes, money into helping Ron Jacobs belongs to the history of our friendship. He had boundless energy and ideas, but I credit myself with providing RJ much-needed guidance to help focus his communications efforts online. I reprinted some of his commentaries to expanded the audience for him. One example follows next.

"The Birth of Boss Radio" by Ron Jacobs

It couldn't have happened if Glen Campbell's manager's wife's father didn't own a cabin at Lake Arrowhead in the early '60s. Eventually, those circumstances brought Bill Drake to Los Angeles as Program Consultant to RKO General's floundering KHJ Radio. And yours truly as Program Director.

Historically, the place to start would be "The Battle of Fresno" which began in 1962. The town's #1 station, pulling 60% shares in the C.E. Hooper ratings, was KYNO, operated by Gene Chenault. It was the only Top 40 station in the market. (In those days "CHR" meant "Career Home Runs.")

It All Started at a 5000-watt Radio Station in Fresno

I was Programming VP of a two-station group which had bought KMAKe in Fresno. After setting up K/MEN in San Bernardino in March 1962, I left it in the hands of PD Bill Watson, and headed for the "Agribusiness Capital of the World." Frank Terry and I towed a U-Haul, full of mostly jazz LP's, through the Tehachapi

Mountains to a small, brick building on McKinley Avenue in Fresno.

Our target was KYNO and we threw everything at them. Terry's Drum-A-Thon was the biggest thing in San Joaquin Valley radio history. KYNO relied on money giveaways. We did our thing, "Circus Radio," which had made K-POI in Honolulu and K/MEN in "San Berdoo" #1.

Gene Chenault did not take this lying down. After a few short-term PDs, Chenault brought in a tall, soft-spoken Southerner working in Stockton. He was previously at KYA in San Francisco, until a new, diminutive owner arrived who couldn't handle looking up at 6-foot-5-inch Bill Drake.

We fired our guns, and KYNO kept a'comin,' now with Drake in command. KMAKe began with me in morning drive (my only airshift in ten years in California), Frank Terry middays and an Army veteran from KMBY, Monterey in the afternoon. He was so good he was moved to mornings within months. His name was Robert W. Morgan.

Drake had Gary Mack and Les Turpin with him, along with the late K.O. Bayley and others. And Gene Chenault's checkbook.

KMAKe started a contest with a $1500 cash jackpot. Before I

parked in my garage KYNO was on the air with a $2000 prize. KMAKe hid a "Golden Key" worth $2500 — KYNO scattered duplicate keys all over town. We tailed Drake in unmarked cars with radiotelephones, trying to catch him doing funny stuff at motels at 3:00 a.m. (Never did.)

KMAKe launched a Bowl-A-Thon with 5-foot-6 inch Tom Maule, KYNO responded with their own, featuring the ominous 6-foot-3-inch Bayley. (KMAKe won that round with some schemes which would make "Tricky Dick" Nixon blush.)

"The Battle of Fresno." It lasted two years. And, of course, there were no "Programming Guidelines" on how to handle the assassination of a President. Generally bummed, and with no company support, I threw in the towel and headed home for Honolulu in early 1964.

Pirate of the Pacific Rim

I wasted a year in Hong Kong working on a "pirate" station which never signed on. This was followed by a month in the Halawa Jail for possession of three milligrams (3/1000th of a gram) of "marihuana."

24 hours out of the cooler, back in L.A. in early 1965, Morgan told me that the Drake-Chenault consultancy, formed after KYNO's

victory, had taken KGB to #1 in San Diego, a Top 40 merry-go-round city. And soon they would take on KHJ, Los Angeles, going for all the marbles. Morgan had signed on as morning man, since polishing his act in Sacramento and San Francisco. He touted a Hollywood native, who called himself The Real Don Steele, to Drake, who hired him for afternoon drive.

Morgan was at his manic best, screaming at me to "Call Drake! Call Drake! You gotta be the PD! Goddamnit, call Drake!" Now understand, 30 days in Halawa Jail wasn't exactly a Super Bowl corporate bash. Low Esteem City.

Besides, Drake and I had never even met. We eyeballed each other once at the 1962 Fresno County Fair. KMAKe displayed "Sunny Jim" Price living in, and broadcasting from, a car hanging 85 feet over the fair grounds. KYNO offered a primitive Darth Vader-look-alike called "The Money Monster" handing out cash. (Advanced students will spot the genesis of "The Big Kahuna" here.)

"Call Drake!" kept ringing in my ears. I was broke, staying with my first wife and a Kowloon alley cat, out in San Bernardino with Bill Watson and his wife, Jodie, an angel. I called Drake. He didn't hang up.

Winky Poos and the Future of Rock 'n' Roll Radio

Within 24 hours, I met Drake and Chenault for lunch at a La Cienega Boulevard restaurant. Our meeting ended and they told me to call Drake's pad at 7:00 p.m.

I couldn't handle the suspense. I phoned Morgan. "This was your big idea, now what do we do?" Morgan came down from his Laurel Canyon cottage, picked me up in his rumpled VW bug and we drove around L.A. in the rain, for hours, listening to KFWB and KRLA.

I repeated, "They won't." Morgan replied, "They will."

Robert W. dropped me at a tall Sunset Boulevard apartment building. Inside I was greeted by Ken DeVaney, who I once met when he was a VP in the hot Crowell-Collier chain. He smiled big - and signaled thumbs up. Drake, Chenault and Turpin were there, along with DeVaney, drinking "Winky Poos."

Chenault announced I was the new PD of KHJ. We celebrated at the erstwhile Cock & Bull restaurant. Chenault toasted Bill Drake and Ron Jacobs as "The two best damn radio programmers in America." I was employed. Hooray for Hollywood!

Almost ten years later, Michael J. Brown, of Brown Broadcasting (KGB, KXOA, etc.) told me: The Rest of the Story. His dad, broadcast pioneer Willet H. Brown, had bought KGB in 1961. It was going nowhere. Mike Brown and his best buddy Roger Adams, Glen Campbell's longtime manager, went skiing at Lake Arrowhead, above San Bernardino. Roger's father-in-law had a cabin there.

Mike, always scanning his car radio, became fascinated with K/MEN. So, when the Browns wanted to make a change at KGB, Mike mentioned the zany "Inland Empire" station to his father, who asked him to check it out.

Mike Brown called the K/MEN office to contact whoever programmed the station. Sheila Brown, the secretary, was out to lunch. So was Bill Watson, the PD. The VP of Programming, yours truly, was in Fresno, fighting a ratings battle in mud and fog. So the K/MEN midday jock grabbed the ringing phone, in this blockhouse in a San Berdoo cow pasture, and blithely told Michael J. Brown that he, the jock, was the programming mastermind!

The deejay, who shall remain nameless (and who used the same first and last name, with an initial in between), was invited to lunch with the Browns at the defunct Luau in Beverly Hills. It took them about the length of a Shirelles record to realize this as a scam. And they were back where they started: KGB seeks PD.

Everyone in the business knew of Willet Brown. He co-founded the Mutual Broadcasting System; hung out with Howard Hughes; owned Hillcrest Motors, your Beverly Hills neighborhood Cadillac dealership; sailed a 93-foot yacht; kept his own Greyhound bus on standby and possessed the world's largest collection of antique motorized popcorn machines.

Gene Chenault, who began as a radio actor, had been trying to reach the senior Brown about a new consultancy spawned by KYNO's success. Meanwhile, while the K/MEN jock turned out to be a flake, Willet Brown decided to find out why Chenault was calling. They met. And Gene Chenault got what he wanted, a client: KGB Radio. Drake, along with Turpin, Maule and others, had the Browns on top in San Diego in 90 days, squashing KCBQ and KDEO. Bill Drake was riding in a long, black Cadillac Fleetwood sedan.

Thomas F O'Neil owned RKO General, Inc. Los Angeles radio was an embarrassment within the company's broadcast division. WOR was a New York giant. WHBQ, Memphis, played Elvis Presley's first record and was an established winner. The other stations were holding their own.

In 1965, O'Neil conferred with his confidant and associate, Willet Brown. He quickly learned of the KGB success story and asked if Brown thought Drake-Chenault could tackle The Bigtime, L.A.,

with their rock 'n roll format. Yes, said the savvy 60-year old.
And the rest is history.

Give Him a Shot

Just one other episode. When Morgan and I were riding in the
rain, my fate hanging in the balance, Drake, Chenault and
DeVaney were hung up on just one point. They were convinced
Jacobs could do the job, but what about this "narcotics thing." The
man's a convicted felon, just out of the Hawaiian slammer —
Reefer Madness!

Drake looked at Chenault, Chenault at DeVaney (a lawyer),
DeVaney said, "Call O'Neil." Chenault telephoned headquarters.
O'Neil said, "Let me think about it."

Thomas F O'Neil picked up his phone and called Beverly Hills.
Hillcrest Motors had a separate building, fronting Wilshire
Boulevard, called "The White House." It was Willet H. Brown's
working office. (He also had the largest office in the KHJ
building, the one with the shower, but he never came around.)

The two tycoons shot the breeze, or whatever tycoons shoot, and finally, O'Neil asked Brown about, "This Jacobs kid. The marijuana business." Willet H. Brown said, "The guy can program your radio station, that's all that really matters. I say, give 'em a shot."

Understand, I never knew many of these facts until 10 years later when Mike Brown told me about skiing in Arrowhead — the fake PD shtick — the phone call to his dad. Had any of that not happened, I would have never walked into KHJ in April of 1965, to join Betty Breneman, Clancy Imislund (the originator of the phrase "Boss Radio"), Eddie Dela Pina, Bill Mouzis, Art Kevin and others who were already there and believed in us: The cocky newcomers who told anyone who would listen, "We're gonna be #1!"

Five months later, we were.

For WHB, in appreciation. May 9, 1990

Most Memorable Ron Jacobs Statements

One especially memorable response that I received from RJ was in the context of his thoughts regarding The Real Don Steele.

RJ: I think Steele might have even been doing those Friday sign-offs before he got to KHJ. Could've been at KISN in Portland or in San Francisco after that. He brought that, along with his "Tina Delgado Is Alive" shtick along with him to KHJ. And any PD who would mess with those would be nuts.

WG: Right, because that's got to be one of the most unusual and unique things.

RJ: Steele, if you analyze his style, is a terrific minimalist. And therefore, when you do a longer form bit, it stands out all the more. It's just like most people don't appreciate the value of white space in a graphic layout. One time a musician friend of mine said, "The most important thing about the music is the space between the notes." If you transcribed what the Real Don Steele say's in a show, there is not much to it, word wise. But when you combine it with his electric energy, where he puts what he says, and how he conveys what he does, when all of a sudden, he rips out one of those things, it is visceral and transcends just words. Style wise, it's not unlike what is now called "rap." Content wise it goes back to what Col. Parker taught me, which is you don't over expose. If Steele did that sign-off every day, it would be less effective.

WG: Yes, that's right.

RJ: If he did it every hour, it would be less effective. And that was also like what I said going back earlier to each guy has strengths to build on. My concept was to give each guy a shtick so that on the one hand, we had a station consistency formatically, but Morgan's thing was to use the phone, no one else did that. Sam Riddle and Roger Christian were to focus on Los Angeles because they were established there. Steele's thing was to kick ass in the afternoon and move it because people had already had it during the day, and so on and so on. And we worked real hard at that. But it absolutely always equally comes down to a matter of what you leave out.

I will always believe that the competitive world of Los Angeles radio helped shape the lives of the participants involved at Boss Radio KHJ. Ron Jacobs me richly colorful details:

RJ: Drake, me, and the jocks didn't give a damn or think about the future, the influence on radio or anything. We had one thing to do which was to kill and be number one. And I wasn't going to be involved with guys who weren't ready to get in there and commit themselves 24 hours a day to climb that damn mountain, and that's where the big rush is. I mean Morgan and me particularly, man, we didn't believe in taking prisoners.

WG: Very serious business.

RJ: Yeah. On May 25, 1965, after the bizarre Muhammad Ali – Sonny Liston fight, Morgan and I went for a drink. After all, the fight was over in a minute. It was one of the few times I ever went to this record hangout called Martoni's. And Morgan and I got into a screaming match with two guys from KRLA. And it almost got out of hand. We all were thrown out of the restaurant.

I mean we took that stuff real serious. And we were really young and we had a lot to prove. We had to prove ourselves to the people in our own building, the Channel 9 people. There were people who had worked in that building who had watched KHJ Radio change formats like diapers.

The engineers siting on the other side of the glass, they'd seen platoons of jocks come and go. So, they just thought we were the format du' jour. Then, when I could sense that we were having some influence on radio in general, I got a perverse joy out of leaving the air studio in the same horrible condition it was in when I first got there.

Guys would fly in from Cleveland, Omaha, wherever, to come and see what the secret thing was that made KHJ work. First, he'd sit in the drab lobby, not a clue that any rock 'n' roll was going on. Then walk down cement hallways that looked like an old Navy building. And he would walk into the control room and there would be this old engineer and a board with pots, right? It could have been a guy with his ham radio.

The only thing I ever did in the studio was have a wooden frame built with a Lucite panel to hang up 5×7 cards for one-liners. And these out-of-town guys, who acted like they're going to the Vatican or the Wizard of Oz–. They'd come in and see a jock sitting there in this 20-year-old room. It had one switch for a microphone and a beat-up turntable that they could listen to the records to on cue, which took a year to negotiate with the union.

If someone asked how we did "it," I would point at my head and say, "Hey man, this is showbiz. What KHJ is doing is not based on equipment or any of that stuff, it's based on this little thing called imagination." That's what I learned from Colonel Parker, it's what I have always preached, and that's what I have always gotten off on. I can do the mechanical stuff, formatics, scheduling. I'm a Virgo, I can do numbers and letters and color-coding. A part of me is really into that. The other side is like, "Wow, what do you do next that people are guessing about."

My theory on the air used to be, they'll listen if they don't know what you are going to do next. That finally comes out almost word after word in the Howard Stern movie. Well, I was doing that stuff when Howard Stern was in grade school, or whatever.

I mean, after doing a high school show, I first got paid as an announcer when I was 18. I was a program director for the first time in 1958, when I was 20. And by wonderful, fortuitous circumstances, I was at KPOA, where we were running "Lucky Lager Dance Time," which was programmed by an ad agency guy named Bill Gavin—and the three-station group had Mike Joseph as their consultant.

It was a great time to learn from guys who were really the pioneers of Top 40, along with Storz and McLendon. And I stayed in contact with Colonel Parker for 40 years. Tom Moffatt and I were honorary pall bearers at his memorial service in Las Vegas. The mechanics were the cake, but The Colonel showed me how to whip up the frosting.

WG: A lot of people really worked together well as a team at KHJ.

RJ: There are so many people that deserve credit. Ed Dela Pena, the chief engineer, and the way we were able to integrate our engineering department and our programming concepts, that's a whole story. The fact that the TV station eventually not only settled down, but realized that interaction would help us both. We came up with a tremendous TV show. That's another thing we had going. No other station in town had their own weekly TV dance show.

WG: That was Sam Riddle's show?

RJ: Yeah. Sam Riddle had a show but that was replaced by the show called, 9th Street West.

WG: That's right. I remember seeing that when I was a teenager.

RJ: It was a great promotional vehicle. I mean, the Big Kahuna would go on and do his thing. And in those days, there were no music videos. Artists and record companies were anxious to be on the number one station and the TV show.

We had an exciting scene going. Like, in the summers of 1965, '66 and '67, not only was LA the center of the rock 'n' roll universe, but KHJ was the pulse of it.

You could drive down Hollywood Boulevard on a Friday night and with your car windows open and it was like just the this wonderful, AM, bass-booming sound. Boss Radio! Everybody was plugged in. It was just wonderful. In the beginning, it seemed like Sonny and Cher were living at the station. Brian Wilson or one of the guys would come up to the entrance at ten o'clock at night and hand the guard a vinyl, and it would turn out to be something like *Good Vibrations* or *California Girls*.

Those years will always be special. I have done other things that have been wild on other levels, okay. But to be there, sitting in the front row of the Hollywood Bowl when Bob Dylan played something electric for one of the first times. Watching The Doors grow from a neighborhood band to a Jim Morrison cult nowadays—know what I mean?

WG: Yeah.

RJ: To see the Big Kahuna go to Dodger Stadium and see the whole crowd turn away from Sammy Koufax to see this silly thing in feathers. It was a rush, man. Like they have "fantasy baseball" and "fantasy football," I would love to be able to take my best or our best hour of KHJ, and put it up against WABC's best hour. Because no one's ever going to convince me that we weren't the greatest rock 'n' roll AM station in the world.

The maintenance of the Boss Radio format would not have been possible without one essential invention–the telephone. Ron Jacobs explained why.

WG: The role of the telephone seems to have played a big role in Boss Radio.

RJ: Well, it was actually pretty cool to have a car phone. That was one of the best status symbols there was in those days. I mean the hippest bachelors drove along Sunset Strip in the car, talking on the car phone. You pushed-to-talk on microphones like a police radio. But the thing looked like a phone that was mounted on the hump between the front seats. And if I heard something happening when I was driving around, I didn't hesitate to call in.

The other side of that coin is the way things get totally blown out of proportion over time. I've been told by second and third and fourth hand people that the hot line was ringing all the time, at least at KHJ. Well, that's a crock. I mean I spent a long time as jock before I did that gig. And I know that in most cases, it's not very productive to hassle someone during their shift.

I would call Morgan when I had an idea in the morning, because we could communicate so well and he could always implement what I suggested if we agreed it was worth trying. Morgan would always come up with what I imagined, or improved on it. Most times I talked to a guy after his shift or sent a memo to him.

WG: Yeah, if you disrupt him in the middle of something and it wrecks the whole pace. Time magazine wrote something about Drake having all those phone lines and calling in all the time.

RJ: Well, Drake had phone lines that he could listen to stations on, but Drake very rarely ever called a Boss Jock on the air. I don't remember that during the time I was at KHJ, that Drake maybe called the jock more than a dozen times. If he did, it might be just to say that sounded cool. I mean, because that's not the way that things work. No one can deal with two different people calling the shots.

Drake would call me no matter what hour of the day. And I would deal with it depending on what it was, like talking to the guy after a shift when he got out of the booth, asking him to come into the office, or sending him a memo, you know what I mean?

One of the real joys of KHJ was that we had what I consider in a lot of ways the best all night guy ever, Johnny Williams. Not only he was great and consistent sounding on the air and a good guy, but I knew that I could go to sleep at night and not get phone calls like I had in the past when someone had taken a Volkswagen apart and put it together in the K-POI big main studio. Or the studio walls were covered with eggs that people were throwing around, partying in the middle of the night. Or people were arriving in the morning and finding someone lying in his own puke.

Top 40 radio had to learn by experience how to cover news events. Two examples of overwhelming news events are the murders of President John Kennedy and his brother Senator Robert Kennedy.

WG: When you were in Fresno, JFK was assassinated. You refer to the fact that a Top 40 radio station had "no guidelines" for how to handle this.

RJ: The assassination of [John] Kennedy to us who were essentially young guys—I mean in '63, I would have been 24-25—was such an incredible surprise, shock, and astonishing event just as a citizen.

WG: How did you guys deal with that at the radio station?

RJ: To have been responsible for what went on the air when, you know, you had a news commitment that you were responsible for as well as religious programming–. In the first place, when John F. Kennedy was shot, it was the first time I had ever seen a wire service machine actually say, "Flash," which you had always heard was going to happen.

The second thing is those days the stories always used to be punched in by teletype operators and there would be a perforated strip of what they had typed. And the reason those machines always clattered constantly is that the strip was usually thirty seconds or so ahead of what was feeding down the line. When the information came in about Kennedy, we stood over the machine and one or two letters would come out and then it paused.

And it was like, there was no CNN. I mean we just huddled over the machine. And then finally when the word came in, which I think the first one was a priest had just come out and said that Kennedy has been given his last rites. I just had to suppress what I was feeling personally because I was really an admirer of JFK. So, to read that bulletin and then play *Peppermint Twist*—I don't know. We grabbed whatever was in the building, which was probably a Mahalia Jackson or a Mormon Tabernacle Choir record and put it on as "appropriate music."

And as a person I remember thinking to myself, well, ha, with all this forensic stuff they have these days at the FBI, at least this will be resolved unlike the Lincoln assassination, which in 1963 was still controversial. How ironic that was. Like, the real truth, at least in my opinion, about the JFK assassination, is still being suppressed.

There is one thing that I regret not having kept from that day. There are a lot of things I did in radio that I don't have, but that's okay. But on November 23, 1963, I wrote an editorial in which I said that it might take a long time to get to the bottom of this, but eventually history would record the truth. I actually tried to make a statement. Probably Robert W. Morgan read it and we replayed it with somber music and that's about all that we could do. We canceled the commercials.

And then finally I was able to go home. And then just maybe when things got normal, you saw Lee Harvey Oswald get shot by Jack Ruby on black and white TV. I mean, I don't want to let my personal feelings about the Kennedy assassination get into it, because I don't think we've been told anything about it that is even close to the truth. But at the time, dealing with it was totally new ground.

WG: In one of your emails you mentioned that you thought being in LA at KHJ was "Camelot" from 1965 until 1968. Bobby Kennedy was assassinated in LA in 1968, and that must not have been easy to deal with.

RJ: The thing that hit home about Robert Kennedy was that one of his campaign headquarters was right across Melrose Avenue from KHJ at Lucy's El Adobe Cafe. And that had been a place for local and visiting Democrats who would come in limousines, coming in and out of there.

There are at least two other historical footnotes I want to mention about that restaurant on Melrose Avenue across from KHJ: Lucy's El Adobe Cafe is also where California Governor Jerry Brown could be seen with Linda Ronstadt when they were dating. Second, director Roman Polanski's late wife, Sharon Tate, along with a few of her close friends ate dinner at Lucy's Ed Adobe Cafe just hours before they became the victims of mass murder at the hands of Charles Manson and his cult.

After Ron Jacobs left KHJ in 1969, he formed Watermark, from which the legendary "Cruisin'" series of record albums and the famous "American Top 40" countdown with Casey Kasem originated. Jacobs also produced several other record albums for Elektra, including the cult classic *A Childs Garden of Grass: A Pre-Legalization Comedy*. He subsequently returned to rock and roll radio programming at San Diego's KGB.

In 2001, Jacobs used the Internet to express his opinions in a "Call to Action" to criticize Randy Michaels, who was at the time the radio CEO of Clear Channel. Later that year, Jacobs used a site named Balance Radio Broadcasting as a platform for his views about Clear Channel. But the site lasted only a few months before being pulled following a controversy over telephone calls between Jacobs and Randy Michaels that appeared online in MP3 form. The legendary Ron Jacobs anger was crystal clear in those recordings.

In 2007, once again the renowned anger surfaced online. Jacobs wrote a commentary on Don Barrett's www.laradio.com in which Jacobs voiced his opinions that too much credit for the success of Boss Radio has consistently gone to other people besides himself.

What was it like interacting with Ron Jacobs?

I have been asked that question many times since the 1970s. This book provides me the first opportunity I have ever taken to give a full answer.

As I mentioned, I met him face-to-face for the first and only time in 1975 at his home in La Jolla, California. I was only a kid of 25 years of age the day I met with him—he was 38 at the time—to record on tape his recollections and comments about Boss Radio.

I was the quintessential "outsider" (I did not work with him at KHJ) but he and I considered each other as friends starting in 1975. I maintained contact with RJ by telephone and email until his death in 2016.

Over the decades, he confided in me many things over the phone that I later wished he had not. I accepted as a basic truth that

RJ was, as the cliché says, **in touch with his feelings**. I remember one most stunning trait was that RJ was able to express his anger to me very clearly.

But, the most disturbing thing that he ever told me was not rooted in anger. He told me that he had become estranged from his adult daughter Miki'ala Jacobs. He admitted that he regretted never having had the opportunity to meet his grandson, Max.

Those unresolved family issues seemed to be the source of deep emotional pain that RJ felt as a father. I urged him to write about how and why the estrangement with his daughter had happened. I believe that men, especially, benefit emotionally from writing about their memories and their feelings. But, RJ was clear with me that he wanted nothing to do with putting such things into writing.

RJ also confessed to me that he felt greatly saddened each time he thought about his contemporaries from the radio business who had died. Of course, that is a normal part of growing older. We all know that. Several times RJ voiced his doubts with me that he, himself, would survive past his 70s. I interpreted what he said to me about growing older in the same context of that famous song, *Ol' Man River* by Jerome Kern and Oscar Hammerstein II from Show Boat: **"...tired of living, but scared of dying..."**

Unless you happen to work in the music or motion picture or broadcasting industries, you will have no idea about what kind of personalities exist and flourish there. But, you probably have seen fictional portrayals of Hollywood egotism such as in Ryan Murphy's 2017 television series *Feud* which depicted the behaviors and battles of Bette Davis and Joan Crawford.

Yes, Ron Jacobs had one of those legendary Hollywood egos that certainly would make for a lot of on-screen drama if anyone ever were to choose to make a movie or television series that included depictions of him. This revelation will not be news to anyone who knew him or had any contact with him.

Interacting with RJ as I did over the phone and via email spanning many years proved to be very unique among all phone calls I have had in my entire life. I found it especially challenging to deal with his shouting at me over the phone. He also threatened me with litigation a couple of times, but never followed through to bring any legal actions against me. However, ultimately, I confronted him with his shouting at me over the phone. RJ shouted at me and replied, "I may be shouting, but I'm open-minded." Comments like that made his famous sense of humor irresistible to me.

I developed a simple coping mechanism for my interactions with RJ. I watched my caller ID and if I saw that an inbound call was coming from area code 909 in Hawaii, I could choose not to answer. Listening to an angry voicemail message from Ron Jacobs could be even far more disconcerting than being yelled at by him during a phone call, however. So much for my simple coping mechanism. I'm sure that there are people alive today in California and Hawaii who would describe their interactions with RJ using very similar (if not identical) words.

If I had not wanted to do websites or eBook production work for RJ multiple times, I would never have done so. He proved to be one very rough haul after another on all the projects that we worked on. At the same time, I doubt that I will ever again have the unique opportunity to interact with someone so smart and innovative as he certainly was.

When I attended the April 16, 2016 tribute to Ron Jacobs that has held in North Hollywood, I was very surprised at how many people in attendance that day openly admitted that they had never actually met him. Yet, each of them spoke so glowingly about him as if he and they were the best of personal friends. That pissed me off. But, I suppose it was merely "a Hollywood thing," so to speak. In my anger, I kept my mouth shut and did not speak in front of that gathering. I was there to honor the memory of Ron Jacobs, not to draw attention to myself. In my head, I was haunted by the sound of his familiar raspy voice shouting at me from beyond the grave: *"Woody, don't you dare fucking get up there in front of that group of strangers to tell shit stories about me!"*

Lessons Learned

When I look back at my connections to the radio business, it is painful for me to admit how I had dreamed as a young man of a long and prosperous career in radio broadcasting. That never happened, however. I have enjoyed working as a producer of eBooks for other people in the radio broadcasting industry. It all started when I guided RJ in the successful navigation of the often-treacherous waters of eBook production and marketing using accompanying websites.

Those of you who may think that all you need do is type up a Word document and push a button to upload the document to Amazon are mistaken! There are many unforeseen roadblocks that you will encounter on your way to getting your eBook up on Amazon.

My reinvention and rebranding has solidified over a short period of time. Following the success of my work producing the eBook for Ron Jacobs, I went on to provide the same professional eBook creation and production services on a one-on-one basis to others who had also worked within the radio broadcasting business in Los Angeles:

Chuck Blore: 2012 Kindle eBook, *Okay, Okay, I Wrote the Book*

Don Barrett: 2013 Kindle eBook, *Adventures in Airtime: Personal Stories of USA Radio People*

Patrick Kelley and Melody Rogers: 2013 Kindle eBook, *And There Will Always Be Termites*

Elliot Field and Anita Garner: 2014 Kindle eBook, *Last of the Seven Swingin' Gentlemen*

You really can never know for certain how things will turn out in your life, so I advise you to do like I did and keep your mind and your eyes open for opportunities to reinvent and rebrand yourself on an ongoing basis as you grow older. Don't be satisfied to be (as Paul Simon called it) a "one-trick pony."

Over the years since my online writing about Boss Radio KHJ became more widely known, I was contacted via email by Paul Drew, Clancy Imuslind, Hank Landsberg, Ken Levine, Gary McDowell, Ramona Palmer, and Bill Mouzis, who each provided me with updated details that I could share online with their permission.

Using the internet to communicate about Boss Radio KHJ has helped preserve the relevance of both the station and the format. Other nonfiction writers have produced similar works on the subject of what happened within radio programming at other radio stations. What eyewitnesses and participants told me about Boss Radio KHJ and the subsequent Drake-Chenault radio programming efforts has become more significant since their deaths if only since I preserved what they had to say. The greatest lesson I took from all this is: Be very careful and very precise if you research and write about people and events in recent life; you just may end up being the only one who safeguards knowledge that otherwise would be forgotten.

Chapter 10:
The Legends and the Mystique

In the late 1950s when he worked in Atlanta on radio station WAKE, Philip Yarbrough adopted the use of the name Bill Drake to rhyme with the station's call letters. It came to be a name representing both myth and reality—a mix of rumors, contradictions and power. I first met the man called Drake in 1973 when he and his business partner, Gene Chenault, took control of that underperforming FM station on Sunset Boulevard. Philip Yarbrough lived 71 years. He died from lung cancer in Los Angeles on November 29, 2008.

When Gene Chenault died in 2010, his grandson, Ryan Moore, told me that Chenault's 90 years represented "an amazing and adventurous life." My perception was that Chenault spoke softly and in so doing carefully concealed his keen savvy and vision about how to bring about financial successes in the radio broadcasting business.

In the formative decades of the 1960s and 1970s within the highly competitive American broadcasting business, I saw how it was entirely common to find people who were single minded, and who unashamedly displayed their self-serving egotism and arrogance. I believe that Chenault stood as a rarity for choosing to do business using his preferred mode of civility and savvy.

The worst that I saw in Chenault was that he would at times use his hearing loss to manipulate a conversation: He might pretend that he didn't hear something you had said to him. That gave him power over you. But, it also gave you time to rethink and restate.

In my opinion, the true legacy of Gene Chenault is that he skillfully hired people who worked closely and loyally with him to realize his personal and corporate goals of long-lasting domination of radio programming.

Drake explained to me in my 1975 interview that getting the RKO consultancy contract ten years earlier gave him and Chenault their first major market proving ground for their particular radio programming concepts. Drake expressed strong praise for Ron Jacobs, who had been selected to be the quintessential program director at KHJ for the launch of the Boss Radio format in 1965; Drake called Jacobs "the best program director I've ever seen."

Accomplishments

In 1990, Drake was interviewed by the *Los Angeles Times* about the 25th anniversary of the Boss Radio format at KHJ. He evaluated the contributions of his team this way: "We cleaned up AM radio. We put everything in its place. It was radio that was designed for the listener. Before us, disc jockeys would just ramble on incessantly."

In 2004, during a rare LA radio interview on KRTH-FM, Drake articulated the importance of that famous radio format directly and with few words: "People tune in to hear the music."

In 2006, Drake was quoted online as offering this explanation: "The REAL key to radio programming, is what you DON'T play…Anybody can come up with a list of songs to play…those lists are everywhere…What to leave IN and what to leave OUT is the REAL secret…and few people have that gift."

The success of Boss Radio and all of the descendant formats that were developed by the Drake-Chenault team in the years following 1965 gave Drake the kind of power mystique that is usually reserved solely for motion picture or political celebrities. He was called an "all-business bachelor" by Time magazine in

1968, and his power and influence was the subject of speculation by trade magazines and the mainstream media.

One Improbable Interview

By the 1970s, Drake had decided that he would no longer do interviews. Yet, Drake agreed to a 1975 interview with me. I was very low on the totem pole and hardly had any interaction at all with Drake while I worked at KIQQ. But, he did know me, and for reasons I'll never fully understand, he agreed to talk with me on the record about Boss Radio and Drake-Chenault radio programming at his home in Beverly Hills.

As we sat near the deep end of his shimmering swimming pool, he tried to explain to me why he had stopped doing interviews. There I was, interviewing Bill Drake at his expensive-looking home in a chic neighborhood in Southern California. Fortunately, I recorded the interview on audiotape because if I'd had to take notes in that moment, I'm sure that I would have failed due to feeling so overwhelmed by the experience of meeting him person.

It felt as though literally I was no longer in my own body, but I was flying somewhere in the sky. I watched myself from an elevated position looking downward seeing myself sitting there next to the famous radio programmer Bill Drake poolside in

Beverly Hills! This was a pinnacle moment in the LA radio adventures of a young, former college radio guy from a "nowhere small town."

Myths versus Reality

The legendary Bill Drake mystique itself was a creation, an invention that grew out of the "Hollywood flavor" surrounding KHJ radio in Los Angeles in the 1960s and continued into the financially successful Drake-Chenault Enterprises projects through the 1970s. The real life Bill Drake—a very tall, well-groomed, polite, Southern gentleman—differed from his well-crafted corporate persona.

Ramona Palmer was married for seven years to this Southern gentleman. She generously shared her memories and photographs from her marriage to him, which you can view at www.bossradioforever.com if you wish.

She explained to me that what we came to know as Boss Radio had roots dating all the way back to when he worked in Atlanta during the late 1950s to 1961: "WAKE had an incredible sound, of course. I would say this was really the starting point for Boss Radio. He just kept honing and improving the format so that when he hit other markets like San Francisco, Fresno, San Diego, etc., there was no turning back. And when he got to Los Angeles and KHJ, he was ready! I did go down to LA when it hit the air and talk about excitement! I was amazed at the sound. I thought the other stations that he had programmed sound good, but nothing like this. It was unbelievable. Everything just melded together perfectly. The jocks were awesome, the jingles were perfect; the newsmen were great. I was so proud of all of them. The rest is history. I do not think there will ever be another station like it. It was, indeed, the best ever."

The power that Drake had was the subject of a lengthy 1969 *True* magazine story: "Most professionals in broadcasting agree that Bill Drake is the most powerful man in American radio today," writer Gene Lees explained. "He is also the most powerful figure in American popular music. Record manufacturers, singers, songwriters, music publishers, all depend on 'air play' to make their wares into hits. Drake says that he doesn't play favorites. His company, he says, programs only records that the public wants and that fit into his own conception of good programming."

The story also noted how in Los Angeles on KHJ "Drake began hammering on a slogan of 'Much More Music,' backing it up by playing more records per hour—14 of them—than the competition." Drake is quoted as saying that he cut down on the amount of air-personality talk to make room for more music. "I tell them, if you want to say something clever, say it in 15 seconds."

Notably, however, it was pointed out in the story how "Drake also cut the number of commercials per hour, on the theory that when listenership goes up and the station can raise its advertising rates, the station would earn more money from fewer spots."

A 1968 *Time* magazine article was entitled "The Executioner" because of Drake's power to fire on-air personalities who did not measure up. This seemed to me to be mainly an exaggeration, but it sure made for appealing newsmagazine copy. The reason for the success of the Boss Radio format at KHJ was explained in some detail in the article: "Once new jocks are hired, they are drilled for a couple of months in the Drake style. The big idea is to unclutter and speed up the pace. The next recording is introduced during the fadeout of the last one. Singing station identifications, which sometimes run at oratorio length elsewhere, are chopped to 1½ seconds on Drake stations. Commercials are reduced to 13 minutes, 40 seconds an hour—almost one-third less than the U.S. average. Newscasts are scheduled at unconventional times, such as 20 minutes after the hour. Thus, when the competition is carrying news, Drake-trained deejays run a 'music sweep' (three or four recordings back-to-back) to lure away dial switchers."

"Drake has built a wall around himself," said *True* magazine, "and Bernie Torres (1932 - 2011) is its biggest brick. This is to keep record-promotion men and assorted hustlers from driving Drake to distraction. Drake is a night person who only rarely rises before noon. Part of his staff, including administrative assistant Bernie Torres, a stocky, good-looking type, comes to the house daily. Torres takes the phone calls, usually telling you Drake isn't home. When he recognizes the name as that of someone Drake will talk to, he reverses his position and calls his boss to the phone. At one of his favorite restaurants, he had to lay down the law to the management that he wasn't to be bugged by promotion men while he was eating. To those he admits to his circle, Drake is a gracious host, an agreeable and often quite witty companion. It is hard to find anyone who hates him personally, even among his bitterest critics."

Chapter 11:
Beyond Los Angeles

The implementation of the so-called Drake-Chenault format and imagery grew to be consistent from market to market. *Newsweek* magazine in 1970 noted, "The Drake sound is a deliberately bland, smoothly modulated mixture of pop favorites, and has been so successful in capturing mass audiences that, within the trade, its creator's name is now used generically, like cellophane and aspirin."

This new approach to rock and roll radio formats that was launched on KHJ starting in May 1965 and celebrated in national publications such as *Time* and *Newsweek* proved to be a smashing financial success. KHJ very quickly shot steadily to the top-rated radio station in Los Angeles, giving RKO that return on investment that the company had wanted. The influence of the format soon spread throughout North America as the Drake-Chenault team used the format to program other RKO owned and operated stations. While not all of the RKO Radio stations used the Boss Radio brand name, the format proven in Los Angeles was implemented in San Francisco, New York City, Boston, Memphis, and Windsor, Ontario (a Canadian city that is part of the metropolitan Detroit

KHJ, LOS ANGELES: BOSS RADIO FOREVER

media market.) That same format inspired imitations beyond RKO Radio in markets such as Buffalo, Cincinnati, Cleveland, and Sacramento, just to name a few.

The Drake-Chenault team also began emulating their Los Angeles-based successes for a much wider, national audience as the then-new FM radio business began to grow in the late 1960s. Drake-Chenault emerged as a leader in developing both the technologies and the content to serve the FM side of the expanding radio broadcasting business.

Unlike today, during the 1960s there were no orbiting satellites to permit the live distribution of radio or television programming. The first satellite delivery of an NBC *Today Show* segment happened in early May 1965, but full-time use of satellites to deliver radio, television, and cable programming would be several years in the future. The most cost-effective means in that pre-satellite era to distribute syndicated radio programming was to produce it in a studio, then transfer it to open reel audio tape, and then ship it physically to hundreds of radio stations. Drake-Chenault was a pioneer in this form of radio programming.

Today's more convenient audiocassette tape technology had not yet been developed. But, there was available technology to play open reel audiotapes in a computerized system that diminished the need for a board operator to be on duty at the radio station. Toward the end of 1968, three RKO Radio FM stations, KHJ-FM, Los Angeles (which in the 1990s became KRTH 101); KFRC-FM, San Francisco (which changed call letters quite often, from its original calls to KFMS to KKEE and back again to KFRC-FM); and WROR, Boston (originally WRKO-FM) all switched formats to Drake-Chenault's syndicated programming service called "Hit Parade '68."

However, Drake-Chenault syndicated programming was not always a hit with radio stations. ne early Drake-Chenault format failed. Annie Van Bebber, one of the most singularly influential Drake-Chenault employees in their syndication wing in Southern California, told me about the very unsolid emergence of the "Stereo Rock" syndicated format:

"Drake was never really into that kind of music. Basically, the whole format was put together by myself even though we had meetings with Bill. I don't think Bill wanted that format. I think it was Chenault who did. Chenault started to run a little scared when he saw all these progressive rock stations popping up. He figured they'd better jump on the bandwagon. Drake at the time wasn't into that at all, had no idea about the music. 'Stereo Rock' went on KPHD [in Fresno.] They changed KYNO-FM's call letters to KPHD and at the time they had just bought KXOA [FM in Sacramento, California] with Mike and Willett Brown, so 'Stereo Rock' previewed on those two stations and one other station in

Milwaukee, I think. So, it went on the air and came right off. It was a good format. It's just that Bill was never behind it, so it just didn't last. They just sort of shelved it, tucked it away. It could have worked."

Van Bebber put into perspective why the Drake-Chenault automated radio programming proved to be so successful overall: "You have to remember at the time there was no competition for Drake-Chenault. There was nothing around like it. There were no 24-hour music syndicated services that stations could buy. It was a great thing for a small town to be able to pay $400 to buy the mastermind Drake's format, put on the air, and have these professional disk jockeys for the amount of money and cut their overhead at the stations like that."

Clearly, Drake-Chenault had a central role in permanently establishing FM as the dominant radio medium for rock and roll music across North America. This crucial historical accomplishment often gets ignored because Drake-Chenault usually is remembered primarily for Boss Radio KHJ, which was strictly an AM radio thing.

Hank Landsberg, former director of engineering at Drake-Chenault Enterprises told me the inside story in his own words:

I started at Drake-Chenault in April 1974. The company was small, with maybe 10 or 12 employees. It occupied about half of the third floor of 8399 Topanga Canyon Blvd. in Canoga Park, California. Drake-Chenault was located in Hollywood previously. At one time the business operated using the name "American Independent Radio" or "AIR."

Because I was hired as Director of Engineering, I saw the company from the perspective of the studio operations. The "corporate culture" was fairly informal, Drake-Chenault being a small organization. I was hired by the General Manager, Bert Kleinman. The Program Director was Lee Bailey. There was a record librarian, Val Faulkenbridge.

In 1974, Gene and Bill were concentrating on K100, trying to make it the "FM version" of KHJ, with The Real Don Steele and Robert W. Morgan as evening and morning drive DJs. It never did all that well in the ratings, partly because of its mediocre coverage from Coldwater Canyon. K100 never did cover as well as other LA FMs that had their towers atop Mt. Wilson.

There were two studios in 1974. Studio B had been built at least 4 or 5 years before I got there. It may have been a studio at DCs original location in Hollywood. The second was built by Jim Somich (then the Chief Engineer at K100) in 1973. Both studios were equipped with lots of equipment that had been "imported" from Gene's stations in Fresno, KYNO (AM) and KPHD (FM). In fact, Gene's FM station in Fresno was the "test bed" for many of the Drake-Chenault automated music formats, and it served as the "test lab" for the automation equipment that was developed to run the formats.

Back in the 60's & 70's, automation equipment was "sluggish" and loose! But that didn't matter if you were running a "background music" format, which was all automation was used for in those days. The thought of using reel-to-reel automation to run a tight top-40 format was unheard of.

That's were some Drake-Chenault innovation came in. The problem of loose, sloppy seques was solved by using a "one-second advance" on the 25Hz tones that signaled the end of each song on a reel of tape. Instead of the 25Hz tone beginning at the end of the cut, it was advanced-in by one second, so it "hit" 1 second before the end of the cut. This gave the next tape deck a "1 second head start" to stabilize and come up to speed, which yielded tight seques without any "wow-in".

My first job at Drake-Chenault was to perfect the system for advancing the cue tones, so they'd be recorded exactly one second before the logical "eom" (end of music) point at the end of a cut.

Here's how it was done: Master tapes were recorded using Sony
(consumer) 4-track (1/4-inch) recorders operating at 7.5 inches per
second. We used a separate track for the cue tone. It was not a
25Hz tone, but instead a 1 kHz tone. Since it was on a separate
track, it wasn't audible in the regular audio tracks. The 1 kHz cue
tones were put on at the logical eom point at the end of each cut.
They were not advanced-in yet. Since these cue tones were on their
own track, the studio engineering could re-record them as many
times as needed until each cue was in exactly the right place, tight
up against the end of the song.

Once the master was done, it was duplicated to a convention 2-
track (professional format) tape. The dupe was done in reverse, or
tails-out. The master played from tail-to-head. During this process,
the 1 kHz tone was sensed, and triggered a 25 Hz generator which
mixed in a 25 Hz cue tone wherever there was a 1 kHz tone on the
master. However, the system was designed so that the 25 Hz
generator remained on for 1 second after the 1 kHz tone ended,
thereby "stretching" the 25 Hz tone by exactly one second. When
playing the dupe heads-out (normal), the 25 Hz tones were
advanced exactly one second before the eom point indicated by the
1 kHz tone on the original studio master.

During the day shift, the only studio engineer working was Mark
Ford, who came from KMEN in San Bernardino. He did mastering
of the syndicated formats, as well as produced the famous Drake-

Chenault demo records. Both studios were used during the night shift. Two studio engineers worked from about 5:00 pm until 1:00 am or so: Mike Williams and Kent Randles also did mastering of the syndicated format tapes.

The studio guys produced the masters. I usually made the "sub-masters" (with the advanced 25 Hz cue tones), which were then sent to SuperScope in Sun Valley, California for high-speed duplication. Despite the fact that the station copies were third generation copies, they sounded pretty good. When I started in 1974, we had about 100 clients, and shipped perhaps 300 ten-inch reels of tape each week.

There were 5 "automated" syndicated formats: XT-40 (top 40), Hit Parade (AC), Solid Gold (AC with oldies), Classic Gold (oldies), and Great American Country. Originally, all tapes were "voiced" with either a front-announce or back-announce. Only the recurrent reels were non-voiced. All formats, except Great American Country, were voiced by Billy Moore. The country tapes were voiced by Bob Kingsley. The announcers would come in once each week and record the 'intros' and 'outros' for all the reels that would be produced that week. Then the studio engineers would mix their voice-tracks with the music, which came (of course) from LPs and 45s.

Drake-Chenault's studio engineers were the best. They would spend hours manually editing the tics and pops out of records until they sounded pristine! Many clients thought we got our music from recording studio master tapes....NOT! It all came from vinyl.

A few years later, Drake-Chenault began to offer format tapes either with or without built-in announcers. My next project was to bring all the tape duplication in-house.

In my early days at Drake-Chenault, our programming tapes were high-speed duplicated by SuperScope in Sun Valley. Their quality was usually good, but it was very, very difficult to maintain "phase coherency" on the copies. Phase errors would manifest themselves as "muddy sound" when a stereo FM station was being heard on a mono radio. Since in those days, most listeners were listening on mono radios, maintaining accurate phase coherency was of paramount importance.

In 1975, I determined that we could produce better-sounding tapes by using an in-house "real time" (not high speed) tape duplication system. I built the first system using 9 Crown model SX722 recorders. I modified the machines so we could run them at 15 inches per second, duplicating tapes at double-time. In addition to duplicating the music, the system also inserted the 25Hz cue tones and added the 1-second advance needed for tight segues when the tapes were played back.

Overall, the system worked well. It produced good-sounding copies that were only one generation from the master, not two as was the case with the high-speed dupes. Level set, equalization test, and head alignment tones were duplicated from the master tape to the copies. We aligned the recording heads to each individual reel of tape, to correct for any potential phase errors. After each reel was produced, it was checked on a special "QC" machine to verify that levels, EQ, and phase were within tolerance. We guaranteed phase to within 90 degrees at 10 kHz, a very tight spec that was unheard of in our industry.

The system usually ran two shifts per day, from 8am until about midnight. The first duplicating technician I hired to run the system was Terry Tretta, who ultimately became one of Drake-Chenault's best production engineers. In 1979, Technics (part of Panasonic Corp.) introduced their RS1500 series of "closed loop" recorders. These machines were much more refined than the old Crown decks. Their closed-loop tape path made them very stable, producing much less phase error than the Crown units. We replaced all of the Crown decks with RS1500s, and increased the capacity of the system by installing 24 Technics decks. Running at double-speed, the duplicating system could now produce 24 excellent quality copies each hour.

I am still convinced that those "inexpensive, consumer" Technics RS1500 decks are one of the most reliable, rugged, and accurate tape machines ever built. I designed special "head adaptors" so I could install Nortronics "Duracore" heads, which would last an incredible 3 or 4 years, with the machines operating 16 hours per day, 5 days a week!

By now, Drake-Chenault's client list had grown to over 300 stations, requiring us to ship about 1,000 reels each week! We did this week after week, year after year. In all the years, I was at Drake-Chenault, we NEVER missed a shipping deadline! The current and recurrent reels ALWAYS shipped on Wednesdays and Thursdays, so the new "hits" could air by the weekend. The 3M and Ampex tape sales reps really loved us. We practically destroyed the old hydraulic elevator at 8399 Topanga Canyon Blvd, bringing up thousands of pounds of tape each week.

The Unanticipated Costs of Success

Ron Jacobs was hired to be the KHJ program director starting in 1965. He resigned in 1969 and moved on to other successful projects such as Watermark, which is best known for creating "American Top 40" hosted by Casey Kasem until 2004 when Ryan Seacrest became the host. I consider the fact that Jacobs left KHJ to be one of several unanticipated costs of the radio programming success of the Drake-Chenault team.

Over many decades, Jacobs expressed his unhappiness with the way things turned out for him as program director at KHJ. Jacobs explained why he left KHJ after only four years in that role. This one statement stands as the most succinct explanation Jacobs could ever give about his experiences with Boss Radio KHJ: "I left KHJ when my contract ran out in June 1969 after what I considered getting screwed in the aftermath of 'The History of Rock and Roll,' There were a lot of broken promises."

One can only imagine how very different things might have been for the Drake-Chenault team had Jacobs remained. I wonder if Jacob's exit could have been prevented. Like many others, I personally have worked for organizations in the 21st century that spelled out in writing the reality that the ownership of an individual employee's work and intellectual rights belong to the organization, not to the individual. Signing over to the organization one's individual claim to ownership of a work or intellectual rights is very common, and it usually is spelled out in writing in advance so nobody can claim later that they are surprised or have hurt feelings.

The absence of particular compensation terms or ownership rights that could have been spelled out in a written contract for

Jacobs (and others) as KHJ became success is one crystal clear symptom of the Drake-Chenault team's groupthink. My evaluation is that there was a classic collective mentality within the group that held and emphasized a strong preference for trusting verbal assurances as proof of one's loyalty to, and faith in, the group. You learn to demonstrate your deep trust in the group by going along with what the group wants. If you don't go along, you risk being kicked to the curb. In effect, you give yourself away willingly and completely until it is too late to reclaim what you feel was yours.

The group suffered a major setback in 1973 when RKO abruptly terminated its contract with Drake-Chenault. Bruce Johnson had become president of the radio side of RKO in 1972. As the new head of RKO's chain of radio stations, his prime responsibility was to keep the chain from losing ground to the emerging power of FM stations that were beginning to attract and maintain loyal audiences. This was much like when television became a potential threat to AM radio in the 1950's, it was now 20 years later, and FM posed a looming financial threat to AM radio's stronghold over the American radio audience.

Here's how Bruce Johnson explained the emerging problem: "When I took the job I was told that the basic problem was the ratings of the RKO stations, which had all been dropping like a rock. They were down about thirty percent I guess, chain-wide. The problem was, as a consultant, Bill Drake was not in a position to order changes. The program directors had become very independent. They were doing whatever they wanted to do and weren't taking his advice. That was the reason things were falling apart. Their position was that they should be employees of the company—Drake and Chenault should be employees of the company. Their recommendation was they be made into vice-presidents—Gene in charge of administration, and Bill in charge of programming. And we should also bring on the staff, Bill Watson as national program director and Bernie Torres as Bill Drake's assistant. So that whole thing was presented to me and I said, 'Okay, fine. If that's the problem, let's attack it that way.'" So it was that the Drake-Chenault team became employees of RKO Radio.

During that interview in Los Angeles, Johnson told me that a key issue in the internal corporate friction between the Drake associates and Johnson was the fact that Drake and his associates were working for two companies, RKO and Drake-Chenault Enterprises. "It didn't matter in the beginning. It mattered to me later on when I felt that maybe too much time was being put in over there and not enough with us. I asked Bill at one time, I said, 'Make a decision. It's either us or it's them. You know, if it's going to be both, then it will be 50/50 and not 60/40 or whatever.' That became a problem. We felt we were paying a great deal of money to then American Independent Radio, later, Drake-Chenault Enterprises. We thought we ought to have better service than we were getting. I got a little upset at times that some of the work that was being done by the music director was going to Fresno and other places, and we had a lot of discussions about that."

In 1965 Ken Devaney became the first general manager of KHJ under the new Boss Radio format. He is credited with building upon promotion man Clancy Imuslind's Boss of the Bay promotional phrase for San Francisco's KYA for the promotional name for the Los Angeles format that became known as Boss Radio. In a 1975 interview with me in Fresno, Devaney corroborated that there were tensions in the management side at KHJ that ultimately produced specific consequences:

"I suppose it's like any other organization. The more remote a figure becomes, the more there is a mystique. If I may use the Howard Hughes analogy: Power we understand he has because he controls the dollars; the mystique is a product of his absences. If he was a known quantity, that is to say, a guy who's on the streets daily and making public statements. There is no mystique to Gerald R. Ford or to Ronald Reagan principally because of that fact that they are very visible and we see their failings or the attributes daily—their good qualities and their bad. Well, Drake just wasn't around. And it's very easy once you have that kind of remote position from any given structure to have a mystique. As far as power was concerned, yeah, he had 'life and death' [hiring and firing power] over jocks. I felt some of his activities were not too healthy for the personnel—certain things he would do: his, seeming to me, unwillingness to allow credit, for example, to be accepted by the persons who had developed an idea, but arrogating this to himself."

Devaney also observed, "I've got to tell you: With Ron Jacobs and the staff that I had down there—and I'm not going to try to exaggerate my contributions at all; it was probably minimal—but that's where the ideas were cooked and hatched and developed. And Drake wasn't around."

The tensions grew until in 1973, Johnson canceled the RKO consultancy contract with Drake-Chenault. And so, after eight years of setting in motion highly successful radio programming systems processes on a nationwide chain of major market radio stations that generated a lot of revenue, on one day in Los Angeles, it all came to an end.

Aftermath and Outcomes

There was life for KHJ after Drake-Chenault. But, symptoms of groupthink in Los Angeles starting in the 1960s at RKO Radio caused the team to lose "the spark" or "the magic" that had once enabled them to stay at the top of the radio broadcasting business.

For a dozen or so subsequent years after Drake-Chenault, other programmers who were not connected to the Drake-Chenault team attempted various strategies and tactics in programming KHJ. Some will be remembered. Others will not.

The year 1974 featured one very memorable Los Angeles radio programming event. Superstars of rock and roll such as John Lennon went on the air live on KHJ to "do their own thing" without a format or music playlist. That was an exciting moment for rock and roll radio because it was so unpredictable. I will never forget hearing Lennon joking his way through awkward reading of live announcer copy for KHJ's commercial advertisers! You can listen to recordings of John Lennon on KHJ at www.bossradioforever.com if you wish.

During the 1970s rock and roll radio started losing its once dominant appeal. One person who saw this coming in particular was Jan Basham. She lived until cancer claimed her in 2003. She distinguished herself at Herb Alpert's A&M Records in Hollywood. She is best remembered and respected as the first female executive in the music promotion business in Los Angeles.

Basham was someone with whom I frequently interacted during my time at KIQQ during the 1970s. She was one of my most favorite people in Hollywood because she was honest and forthright. Imagine encountering those particular traits existing in

172

Hollywood! In an interview with me in 1975, her characteristic candor was evident when she expressed her view that by the mid-1970s, the excitement was gone from top 40 radio in Los Angeles. "I'd say it's not exciting as a record promoter or even as a listener. Most of the personalities on top 40 radio are really good, but they all sound alike. Nobody talks about what anybody on the air says today. Nobody cares. Top 40 radio is just really bland right now was far as personalities are concerned. I'm not sure if that's the reason why radio in general has lost a lot of listeners."

The former rock and roll powerhouse KHJ slid into a downward trajectory and the station never again was able to recapture its former status as a pop culture icon. The KHJ call letters lived on until the end of January 1986 when RKO made the decision to change KHJ to KRTH-AM (since their FM station call letters are KRTH-FM). The KRTH-AM call letters lasted through the Smokin' Oldies format after which RKO sold both stations to Beasley, which in turn sold the AM station to Liberman Broadcasting, operators of Spanish language stations KWIZ in Santa Ana, and KBUA and KBUE known collectively as "Que Buena." They turned the former KHJ into KKHJ, which became known as "La Ranchera," but in so doing, the original call letters KHJ were given up.

When the Libermans purchased the station, the closest call letters they could obtain from the FCC were KKHJ. This is because call letters KHJJ were already in use by a station in the San Joaquin Valley calling itself KHJ. But, one problem was that KKHJ could not mention its call letters on the air in Spanish. The reason may not be apparent to those who only speak English.

In Spanish, the letter "K" is not pronounced "kay" as it is in English. The letter "K" is pronounced as "kah" in Spanish. If you say "kay-kay" in English, that doesn't mean anything.

But, when you say "kah-kah" in Spanish, well—. You must have already figured out where this is going! Having station imagery with the word shit in it in any language would be a liability. To compensate for this problem, dating back to its inception, the station call letters were only given in English ("kay-kay-aitch-jay") and referred to on the air in Spanish as "La Ranchera."

In a drive spearheaded by KKHJ Program Director Alfredo Rodriguez and Chief Engineer Jerry Lewine, the station collected letters from listeners and community leaders explaining the problem the station faced. They forwarded those letters to and spoke with staff at the FCC with the request that they make an exception to their policies and permit the station to drop one of the "K's" and return to the call letters that the station had for over 65 years, KHJ.

Under the circumstances, the FCC made a rare exception to the rules and granted the request. As a result, on March 15, 2000, the original call letters KHJ once again returned to Los Angeles.

The Spanish language programming did not survive on the AM dial. In 2014 Liberman Broadcasting bought a Southern California FM station, KWIZ, Santa Ana, and moved the "La Ranchera" brand of programming there. Immaculate Heart Radio Education Broadcasting of Loomis, California purchased KHJ in 2014 and yet another radio format change on the station followed: KHJ started broadcasting Roman Catholic faith programming. *Dominos vobiscum!*

Chapter 12:
The Beginning of the End

Bruce Johnson had very clear opinions about the motivation behind the Drake-Chenault team's efforts in the early 1970s at KIQQ: "In my opinion, the motive of the whole thing was one of revenge. I knew that for a long time; you know they never mentioned KHJ on the air but they said the 'United California Bruce building' [a reference to the former RKO headquarters within the United California Bank Building in Hollywood], and they went on about Paul Drew [then KHJ program director] and did some fairly nasty things on the air to the point that we called them up and told them 'cut it out or we're going to sue you.' The listeners didn't know what the hell was going on—they couldn't care less. So they [K100] really took after us and I felt it was foolish. They weren't going to win anything. They might have hurt us a little bit. They weren't going to beat us. They just kept on and on with this thing and we ignored them."

It was difficult to ignore Robert W. Morgan and The Real Don Steele, however. The pair, whose public images as LA radio celebrities, gave the new K100 a high-energy announcing style that had originally been the hallmark of Boss Radio in 1965. In many ways, "the new K100" seemed to me as an attempted reincarnation of Boss Radio nearly 10 years later. One crucial difference, however, was that the 1973 Drake-Chenault programming on KIQQ did not boost that station to number one in Los Angeles like Boss Radio had boosted KHJ in 1965.

While KIQQ was promoted on the air enthusiastically as "the dawn of a new radio day," ambitiously promising a new future in radio programming, in 1974 Rolling Stone magazine, noted the obvious similarities between the station and Boss Radio by commenting, "After listening to K100 one gets the feeling that the future sounds a lot like the past." Other trade publications at that time reported that, under Drake-Chenault, KIQQ became the only top 40 station to play Bruce Springsteen's *Tenth Avenue Freeze-Out* and Roxy Music's *Love Is The Drug*, and the first station in Los Angeles to play Queen's *Bohemian Rhapsody* and Peter Frampton's *Show Me The Way*. Here's an obscure fact that probably never got mentioned anywhere: I created a stereo version of *Smoke on the Water* by Deep Purple to play on KIQQ because when that song was released as a single in 1973, it was only in mono. Unfortunately, the "dawn of a new radio day" never really was realized, and in 1975, both Morgan and Steele departed KIQQ. That was the beginning of the end. What could have been a Los Angeles comeback for Drake-Chenault radio programming would never happen.

Irving Ivers, the first KIQQ general manager under the original ownership team, told me in 1975, "I think their priorities were all wrong. Between the time they were dumped out of KHJ and the time that they got to K100, the vendetta was beginning to grow and gnaw at them. And I think their priority at K100 was to approach it with a vengeance in order to seek some kind of revenge towards KHJ. Well obviously it didn't happen. It didn't happen because the priority was wrong. They just tried to copy what was already in existence as opposed to trying to come up with something new and different."

In the late 1980s, KIQQ was bought by Westwood One, which changed the call letters to KQLZ, and the station was promoted on the air as "Pirate Radio." Neither those call letters nor that imagery lasted very long. The FM station licensed in Los Angeles at 100.3 MHz has over many years been given so many different formats and call letters that it is difficult to keep track of the changes. If anybody out there reading this is qualified to evaluate whether the karmic debt is still in effect that I helped bring upon LA's 100.3 on the FM dial, please make your presence known to me.

Many of those who contributed directly to what was a huge success in Los Angeles radio starting at KHJ in 1965 have since passed away. Yet, you can still find online discussions about what happened during those glorious days of Boss Radio KHJ, and more importantly, who should be remembered as having had the most important roles.

In 2007, one year before Bill Drake passed away, new discussions about who deserves credit for Boss Radio KHJ were instigated by Ron Jacobs in comments he made via Don Barrett's www.laradio.com website. Drake clearly was angered. He responded by writing a very rare bylined commentary that started with an apology: "I'm truly sorry that after all these years this response became necessary. This mess puts a cloud over some otherwise very fond memories. I find this very unpleasant. And sad. Let's not try to rewrite history. Let it be. My God! That was over 40 years ago."

Why would Jacobs remain angry and hurt about his KHJ experiences? He quoted none other than Gene Chenault to me, who in 1965 speculated what the new team would accomplish starting at KHJ:

"Chenault's point of view that night was that 'Grant and Lee had been brought together on the same team.' And of course, I'm going 'Right on! Which one am I? 'Grant or Lee?' Drake's rap to me that night was, 'This is just the beginning. RKO's got these other radio stations. After we do the job here in Los Angeles, Ron, well then, we'll move on to other things. You'll take the East Coast and I'll take the West Coast.' Or, vice versa—I forget which coast

I was supposed to get." Jacobs got no coast at all. He eventually left the mainland to return to his native Hawaii, where he held on until his death the anger that had reached a boiling point when he was a young man in Hollywood.

Jacobs was bluntly honest with me in 1975 when he told me: "I never felt myself as part of Drake-Chenault. I mean, I always feel I'm working for the people whose name appears on the paycheck. Drake-Chenault was, because of FCC requirements, at least technically not in the line management of the station. They were literally consultants. As they expanded, I had to pretty much restrain my emotions about their success on Xeroxing what myself and others had done at KHJ."

A palpable anger and bitterness on the part of Ron Jacobs towards the team at Drake-Chenault for copying, adapting, and repurposing apparently did not fade with the passage of time. Jacobs articulated his intense feelings to me in 1975—six years after he left KHJ—in unmistakably clear language: "I wasn't spending a lot of time getting off on the fact that Drake-Chenault consultancy had elevated the RKO station in Boston from nothing to everything—except for whatever satisfaction you can get in knowing someone has taken your stuff and doing it at another station…It was important to me that the people that mattered knew and the people, more importantly, that I personally respected intellectually and hung out with knew… From then it got to be downhill. I was probably sublimating my bitterness about it and it resulted in my eventually splitting from there."

Even though he consistently displayed a clear respect in public statements regarding Bill Drake, the passage of time did not diminish the feelings Jacobs had towards how badly he felt the Drake-Chenault team had treated him during the 1960s. "If you were writing about McDonald's," Jacobs explained, "no matter what PR Ray Krock put out in his lifetime, you must remember that the whole deal was a creature of the McDonald's brothers' imagination. Krock cloned it, beyond, I'm sure, his wildest dreams. In this analogy, think of Drake and me as the brothers and Chenault as Krock. Is that metaphor subtle enough?"

In contrast, Drake remembered the start of the collaboration with Jacobs minus anger or drama. He told me that getting the contract to program the RKO Radio chain starting with KHJ was the beginning of the attainment of a goal that he and Gene Chenault had long held. They wanted to program several stations simultaneously as the core of the business strategy. The reality is that their coming to Los Angeles to KHJ and creating Boss Radio was never intended as an exclusive LA deal: "The reason I wanted to get into that in the first place was that I wanted to do a multiple-station thing. At the time we were doing Stockton, Fresno—those were the first two—and San Diego, there were three. Then with the advent of the L.A. thing, I had to drop Stockton, and there were still three. Just trying to put it together, whether it was a station like KFRC [San Francisco] or whether it had been someplace else didn't much matter to us."

In the September 2004 K-Earth 101 interview broadcast in Los Angeles, Drake commented that the development of the radio format for Los Angeles happened as he and others wrote down "…a few things on some bar napkins…" at various venues that served adult beverages.

For his part, Drake was focused on the national expansion that was made possible by the work of the talented team at KHJ. "KFRC was approximately a year after KHJ, sometime I'd say around the summer of '66. I think that CKLW [Windsor, Ontario, Canada] and WRKO [Boston, Massachusetts] and WOR-FM [New York City] at the time, then WHBQ [Memphis, Tennessee] was six months to a year after that, I think. I forget the time. I don't really know, but it was KHJ and then KFRC and then a little later the others." Drake further explained that he entrusted the programming management of KHJ to Jacobs because he believed in Ron Jacobs.

But, there was more to the decision than that. Drake admitted that he, himself "being program director at KHJ was never the intent." When KFRC also succeeded in attracting a large audience as KHJ had done, Drake noted that some critics labeled the Drake-Chenault programming as purely a California phenomenon: "They said at the time after Los Angeles and San Francisco, 'Well, that's West Coast Radio.' You never know, so at that point we'd been approached by a guy from KAKC in Tulsa, Oklahoma. It was good money and also it was a very interesting thing for us because I figured, 'All right, if this is supposedly 'West Coast Radio,' Tulsa is the middle of the Bible belt and home of Oral Roberts and all that stuff.' So, we went into Tulsa and did it, and the same thing happened. We had actually tested [the format] there in the middle of Oklahoma before we did Detroit, Boston, New York, and all that."

During the late 1970s after the attempt at KIQQ to make an industry comeback by successfully programming a Los Angeles radio station proved not possible for them, the Drake-Chenault team and the company bearing their hyphenated surnames shifted focus entirely to the business of radio programming via syndicated services delivered on tape as detailed elsewhere in this book. In 1983, after 21 years as a business partner with Chenault, Drake sold his interest in their company. Shortly thereafter, the company was bought by Wagontrain Enterprises and was relocated from Canoga Park, California to Albuquerque, New Mexico. As satellite-delivered radio programming emerged in the 1980s, the former Drake-Chenault organization and intellectual properties were bought by Jones Intercable.

Chapter 13:
Reaching for the Stars

The business of radio broadcasting changed forever when corporations that own multiple media outlets discovered that they could cut operating costs by using advances in technology that once were literally considered science fiction. Although the radio broadcasting industry started firmly on the ground, the future literally took a giant leap into the heavens, where it remains today.

Arthur C. Clarke invented satellite radio when he was spinning tales as a writer of science fiction. The visionary author of *2001: A Space Odyssey*, which Stanley Kubrick transformed into a motion picture in 1968, envisioned a world in which radio relay satellites in orbit around Earth would deliver instantaneous worldwide programming. Clarke's 1945 short story *I Remember Babylon* predicted a futuristic technological enterprise that took just 30 years to make the jump from the pages of pulp science fiction to the basic bottom line of the American radio business. Clarke turned out to be correct when he speculated that man-made satellites could be "parked" in orbit at a fixed speed that enabled a fixed position far above the planet's surface where receiving and relaying radio signals was enabled.

The use of geosynchronous satellites directly enabled an unintentionally negative use of technology by prominent media corporations: One announcer in one studio in one location can be heard by listeners doing a show live to multiple radio stations across multiple time zones, thus eliminating the need for media corporations to employ individual announcers in all those radio stations. This tangible loss of job opportunities can be directly attributed to the use of technology.

In the early 1980s, some of what was previously unfathomable from a business perspective became reality. Technology changed in the radio business so that even small radio market stations could sound more professional by becoming part of a satellite delivered syndicated radio programming network. But, there was a price to pay. And it has nothing to do with the price of syndicated programming.

During the 1980s, I wrote an article about satellite-delivered syndicated radio programming when it was new. In the process of my research, I interviewed Steve Stagnaro, who was then vice president and general manager of a Santa Maria, California FM station, KXFM, which served parts of both Santa Barbara and San Luis Obispo Counties.

"My first reaction to satellite-delivered radio," Stagnaro told me, "as a programmer and business manager of a station was, 'what a great idea!' We could get a national, good-sounding DJ on the air and save some money. Then, I began to think it has a problem. I discovered that problem by this station once being fully automated."

Fast forward: Radio programming now generates multiple millions of dollars with national on-air talent such as Howard Stern, whose programming reaches listeners because of satellite technology. My guess would be that Stern probably has never experienced small towns in Central California where people live who listen to him. They live on the Central Coast and have no reason to care that Stern's show originates from New York City.

And that's the whole point. A February 25, 2002 page one *Wall Street Journal* analysis of local radio under the control of megacorporation Clear Channel, for instance, quoted its then radio CEO, Randy Michaels: "I don't think it's at all wrong or deceptive to put together terrific programs that reflect local communities and sometimes use talent who may physically be somewhere else." Randy Michaels compared the radio shows to films, which wouldn't be "nearly as much fun if the camera kept turning around to show you it was just a set. I don't know that the radio experience would be as good if we said every five minutes, 'By the way, I'm not really here and I taped this 20 minutes ago.' But that's all part of the magic of creating entertainment."

It also may be significant that in June 1980 National Public Radio became the first American radio network to use satellite distribution on a full-time basis. Then, as now, advertiser support is not what keeps NPR on the air. Perhaps it had to be radio broadcasters who do not rely upon advertiser support to take chances to get satellite technology to cook. NPR began distributing radio programming by satellite in 1979, well ahead of much of commercial radio.

In the years that followed, NPR satellite delivered multichannel programming such as opera, jazz, and fine arts along with public affairs and news programming. That multichannel programming paradigm clearly belongs in our era. Sirius XM Radio has already proven that business model.

But, what does the future hold for localization? And what about radio jobs? Let's go back to the past to seek an answer.

Sam Kopper started a company called Starfleet in the late 1970s to produce and distribute live-by-satellite radio concerts. Emphasizing the national, built-in excitement of a live-by-satellite concert (as compared to a broadcast of a concert taped live), Starfleet dawned as a shining moment in the earliest efforts of satellite-delivered radio.

Any self-respecting *Star Trek* follower knows that the original "Starfleet," of which the starship Enterprise attracts most of the limelight, personifies intergalactic command and distribution of wealth. Kopper's Starfleet consistently commanded more kudos than wealth with concerts featuring a wide variety of artists like Bruce Springsteen, Bette Midler, Hall & Oates, the Charlie Daniels Band, Blondie, Tammy Wynette, and even the Boston Pops.

Kopper sold his network to John Blair and Company, and there was a switch from being a network to being a producer of programming for networks. He admitted to me that he when he talked with me for my satellite radio article that he was concerned satellite radio networks operating on a 24-hour basis would likely jeopardize localization and hurt people's chances of getting into radio careers. "One of radio's great attributes is that it can be local and serve the people right around the radio station," he said. Kopper typified the view in the 1980s that the round-the-clock satellite radio would be the doomsday machine for many who seek local employment in radio. "I think it would be bad for radio— having radio be less localized. I'd hate to see a significant number of people get blown out of chances to get into radio."

Stagnaro explained the essential problem: "KXFM really died when it had no localization, when it was a voice from Dallas, Texas, and music picked from Dallas, Texas, from their view of the United States musically, with no idea that the coast of

188

California and the beach, and our lifestyle here affects the music we like, and the way we like it presented."

"I was forced to take KXFM from a full-automated station to doing our own music in-house," Stagnaro commented, "and get live air talent again on the station to compete locally. I began to wonder ability the ability of a network radio station sitting in some city far away feeding programming to us. I wonder how they could relate to my listeners, for example, sitting out there in Nipomo, California, growing oranges."

Chapter 14:
Cutting the Edge on the
Cutting Edge

Human nature demands that we each have some way to release pressures in our lives. We all need something to cut the edge. The Drake-Chenault team had their adult beverages containing alcohol and nicotine cigarettes in those long-ago days before anyone envisioned opioids like Vicodin and benzodiazepines like Xanax and Valium.

A restaurant and cocktail lounge named Martoni's at 1538 N. Cahuenga Boulevard was a favored Hollywood venue for Drake dating back to the 1960s. Martoni's is long gone now, but anyone alive today who worked in Hollywood 50 years ago certainly will remember the place. The use of alcohol and cigarettes was commonplace in those days, and it was very easy in the 1960s to find photographs taken in Los Angeles showing Drake with others holding a cocktail.

Today, of course, there has been a swing to far more outlandish behaviors compared to the relatively innocent 1960s. Photographs and/or videotape of people who are inebriated in public can easily be found on a regular basis on entertainment television shows such as TMZ. But, 50 years ago, the cultural norms were very different. Among the Drake inner circle at that time alcoholic beverages were affectionately code-named as "winkiepoos" so that any direct reference to booze was avoided. But, the use of alcohol was not only a fact of life in Hollywood rock and roll radio during the 1960s, it was a source of humor and camaraderie.

At the 25th Anniversary of Boss Radio in 1990 in Century City, for instance, you could hear reunited former KHJ employees making joking references to Martoni's, to "winkiepoos," and to being ejected from the premises by the bartender. In response, the audience laughed and applauded.

Ron Jacobs told me: "On May 25, 1965, after the bizarre Muhammad Ali – Sonny Liston fight, Morgan and I went for a drink After all, the fight was over in a minute. It was one of the few times I ever went to a record industry hangout called Martoni's. And Morgan and I got into a screaming match with two guys from KRLA. And it almost got out of hand. We all were thrown out of the restaurant."

The long-term consequences of such basic and readily available chemicals to soothe the pressures of professional life in show business did not have the public awareness then that we do today. The risks of the daily use of tobacco and its promotion of lung cancer—ultimately what shortened the lives of Bill Drake (1937 - 2008), Robert W. Morgan (1937 - 1998), and The Real Don Steele (1936 - 1997)—were just not yet on anyone's radar screen.

Of course, tobacco and alcohol were not the only ways to cut the edge back in the day. Another choice was speed. And no, I am not referring to the recreational drug alpha-methylphenethylamine.

Roger Christian (1934 - 1991) was one of the original seven Boss Jocks on 93/KHJ starting in 1965. He was known for being into cars. Very fast cars. Together with Brian Wilson, Roger Christian wrote car songs like *Shut Down* and *Little Deuce Coupe* that The Beach Boys recorded in the early 1960s. He also co-wrote *Dead Man's Curve* for Jan and Dean. I selected Roger Christian to be the narrator of the 1973 LA radio documentary entitled "The Sgt. Pepper Boys Are Back" that I wrote and produced for broadcast on KIQQ. My most vivid memory of Roger Christian involved a very fast car. One day in 1973, he drove me in his beloved Jaguar from his home up on Mulholland Drive down to the Cosmic K100 studios on Sunset Boulevard. If ever there were a land speed record for traveling down Cahuenga Boulevard, it should've belonged to Roger Christian for that trip! I imagined after miraculously surviving that trip in his Jaguar that Roger Christian would one day go out in a blaze of high-speed glory while behind the wheel of an imported automobile. His life of 57 years ended from complications of kidney and liver problems, however.

Chapter 15: Benchmarks

The date: Wednesday, May 9, 1990. The place: J.W. Marriott Hotel in Century City, California.

The opening night of the *Radio and Records* annual trade magazine convention features a $93-per-person admission price to a reunion party. This is your basic once-in-a-lifetime event. The Johnny Mann Singers are performing the "93 KHJ" jingle live as Robert W. Morgan reaches the podium. A clear sense of anticipation and excitement flows through the audience at the speed of sound.

You are in the presence of Bill Drake, Gene Chenault, The Real Don Steele, Robert W. Morgan, and many other members of the radio and record industry in Los Angeles. Hal Blaine has a full drum set occupying a prominent position to the left of the podium. Johnny Mann, himself, leads his original Singers poised in readiness to the right of the podium. Few people have ever heard a live performance of a KHJ jingle before. So when Blaine, Mann, and the Singers jump into their work, you are helpless with awe.

The recorded voice of Dick Clark booms down upon the crowd and announces why this anniversary is being celebrated at all: No radio station before or since has had such a national impact, says the strangely disembodied voice.

Casey Kasem appears in person, however, representing the historical Los Angeles radio opposition between KRLA and KHJ. He seizes the opportunity at the microphone to deliver a unique tribute by voicing the "93 KHJ" station identification—a phrase you never thought you'd hear him say at any microphone.

You listen to Bill Drake thanking everybody for their hard work in making Boss Radio KHJ as successful as it was, and watch in anticipation as Drake introduces his partner, Gene Chenault, who chooses to remain ever silent in the audience. The ones who say the least probably say little because they are the most powerful ones in this room tonight.

Most of the talking is done by the others. You watch the original Boss Jocks, Robert W. Morgan, Gary Mack, The Real Don Steele, Dave Diamond, Sam Riddle, Johnny Williams, and Frank Terry each take turns at the microphone. Once-secret anecdotes— and outright lies—about sex, booze, drugs, and rock and roll punctuate the memories. If you listen to these guys, there's no way to learn what really happened 25 years ago. The Real Don Steele observes, "Twenty-five years later and we still can't tell the truth!"

Ron Jacobs summed up clearly for me what the major players were thinking while they were making Boss Radio KHJ into the success that it became. He told me: "Drake, me, and the jocks didn't give a damn or think about the future, the influence on radio or anything. We had one thing to do which was to kill and be number one. And I wasn't going to be involved with guys who weren't ready to get in there and commit themselves 24 hours a day to climb that damn mountain, and that's where the big rush is. I mean, Morgan and me, particularly, we didn't believe in taking prisoners."

The rarity of their appearance together here in Century City tonight is really what matters most. Rarest and most special of all at this anniversary party is the appearance by a man named Clancy Imuslind. He does not look boss. He looks dignified, charismatic and spiritual.

It was Clancy Imuslind who coined the Boss Radio phrase as promotion director at KHJ radio in 1965, but here and now, Clancy Imuslind seems out of place, as if he belongs elsewhere—somewhere more important perhaps. He jokes about how, despite all the charitable work he has done, "the one thing I'm remembered most for is Boss Radio!"

The "free and easy" party atmosphere and the rounds of laughter conceal two unmistakable truths, however: The first is that the entire, original Boss Radio team is not reunited here tonight. Robert W. Morgan makes a vague reference to the absence of original Boss Jock, Roger Christian, but Morgan never explains why his former KHJ radio colleague did not attend.

And that points us to the second truth: Living the life of a Boss Jock was neither "free," nor necessarily "easy." Watch the celebrants at the 25th anniversary joking about drugs and alcohol, and you might just see this truth is worn deeply into their faces.

Just over a year later, Roger Christian dies. And then lung cancer cuts short the lives of both The Real Don Steele and Robert W. Morgan less than ten years following the 25th anniversary of Boss Radio.

Jacobs and Drake: The Final Conversation

Other than the 25th anniversary in 1990, the other single most important historical benchmark pertaining to Boss Radio would have to be the 1999 conversation between Ron Jacobs and Bill Drake.

Ron Jacobs was on the mainland to visit his daughter, Miki'ala Jacobs DeVivio, in 1999. While in Los Angeles, Jacobs met face to face with Bill Drake for what would be the last time.

Together they recorded an unusual free-wheeling, candid exploration of their lives in the rock and roll radio business. Tape recordings of the conversations over two days at Candy Canyon bar located in Woodland Hills, California during the month of June 1999 were made. Jacobs preserved the tapes and gave me edited transcripts to reprint with his permission.

RON JACOBS: So, it's 1999, and do you want to tell us about where we are?

BILL DRAKE: This is the world-famous Candy Canyon [bar]. And this is Ron Jacobs and Bill Drake.

RON JACOBS: And is this Topanga?

BILL DRAKE: It's Woodland Hills on Topanga Canyon Blvd.

That "Radio Name"

RON JACOBS: You were born Phillip Yarbrough, so how did you get that radio name?

BILL DRAKE: Oh, it wasn't my idea. You have to realize at that time—back in the late 1950s—companies would go in and buy radio stations. They all would copy one another. But the stations weren't paying anybody any money. So, a guy would go into a market and if he was good, somebody from across the street at another station would offer him more money and hire him. Bartell Broadcasting Company figured a smooth way around this. They assigned everybody a different name and Bartell then owned the name.

RON JACOBS: The company.

BILL DRAKE: Yeah. So, the station I went to work for was WAKE in Atlanta.

RON JACOBS: Which was a big station.

BILL DRAKE: Well, a 250-watt radio station. It was the biggest 250-watt station that I ever saw. We wound up with a 42 share [in the local radio station ratings]. They were going to name me Blake. They wanted something that rhymed with WAKE. So, I said how about Drake? That was my mother's side of the family. Drake.

RON JACOBS: So, the whole thing about San Francisco and the Sir Francis Drake Hotel and all that, is bullshit.

BILL DRAKE: What was that?

RON JACOBS: People say that you got to San Francisco after Atlanta and you changed your name to Drake when you get there. Because of the Sir Francis Drake Hotel in San Francisco. That's bullshit, right?

BILL DRAKE: I've seen that published. A lot of people talking about that–talking about how it actually happened. But, no,

I was Drake in Atlanta from 1958 and then went to San Francisco in 1961.

Georgia Roots

RON JACOBS: So, you grew up in Donalsonville in a corner of the state of Georgia.

BILL DRAKE: I was born January 14th, 1937. In Waycross, Georgia.

RON JACOBS: Not Donalsonville.

BILL DRAKE: No. Waycross. Right at the edge of the Okeefenokee Swamp. Don't you know about Waycross? (Laughs).

RON JACOBS: All the published stuff says that you're from Donalsonville.

BILL DRAKE: Well, that's where I grew up. I mean, I was born in Waycross, and my parents moved from there to Donalsonville when I was like a year old.

RON JACOBS: How far is Waycross from Donalsonville?

BILL DRAKE: A hundred miles. A hundred twenty miles.

RON JACOBS: Waycross is more well known, right?

BILL DRAKE: Well, yeah, anything is more well-known than Donalsonville. Waycross is almost on the coast. The Atlantic coast. Like a little north of Jacksonville, Florida. ''Cause Jacksonville, Florida is in the northeast corner of Florida and then you got that Okeefenokee Swamp and then you got Waycross, Georgia.

RON JACOBS: So, you're born 1937 in Waycross and why were your parents there do you think?

BILL DRAKE: Oh, I guess 'cause my daddy had a job. He was an auto parts guy.

RON JACOBS: And your mom?

BILL DRAKE: She was a schoolteacher. Second grade.

RON JACOBS: Brothers, sisters?

BILL DRAKE: None.

RON JACOBS: Why do you think your parents picked Donalsonville?

BILL DRAKE: Well, they'd grown up around Donalsonville anyhow. My grandfather, Papa Drake, lived five miles from Donalsonville and my father was like fifteen miles from there in Blakely. That's where they met and got married and then my father got a job and they moved to Waycross and that's where I was born.

RON JACOBS: What was your mother's maiden name?

BILL DRAKE: Maxine Drake. But they called her Pat for some reason, I don't know why.

RON JACOBS: Where did that side of your family come from?

BILL DRAKE: The Drake name supposedly they have traced it pretty much back to Sir Francis Drake, who was a fucking thief and a pirate. On the Yarbrough side of the family—the Yarbroughs I don't think anybody had inspected them too carefully. I'm not sure they wanted to know. But the Yarbroughs were all from that area of the country. From all around the state of Georgia. But from what I was told as a kid, I never paid attention to that stuff. But they were talking in English and German.

The Day FDR Died…On the Radio

RON JACOBS: When do you think that you can first remember hearing the radio and what was on it?

BILL DRAKE: Well, I remember listening to the radio as a kid but it was just sort of there. I was amazed by it. It astounded me the day that Roosevelt died. To me, up until that point in time radio was just a box that talked and there was music in it and I never paid that much attention to it. But, I remember that my grandparents and my mother who were the strongest people I knew. I remember that particular day. I went in to the house after playing outside. The radio was on and I heard: Franklin Delano Roosevelt had died in Warm Springs, Georgia [April 12, 1945]. And everybody went ape shit.

RON JACOBS: How far were you guys from Warm Springs?

BILL DRAKE: Well, it was a hundred and fifty miles or something like that. But, that wasn't the thing. The thing that amazed me was that the radio, which I'd never thought that much about before, could absolutely and totally destroy the three strongest people that I knew. And I thought to myself, what the fuck is that? Having no idea that it was because of Roosevelt and that it was a once in a lifetime occurrence. All I knew was that whatever happened, it was because of that damn radio. My grandparents and my mother went fucking nuts.

RON JACOBS: In my mind, the radio could connect us on the little island in the Pacific to the mainland. And it was more of a communications thing. But what's interesting in your experience was radio was this inanimate object and it could have such emotional impact. It was all of a sudden impacting these people who were the strongest people you knew. So, when this radio impact happens, you learn that the box becomes this thing that could carry emotion.

BILL DRAKE: Well, I was intrigued but I couldn't figure that out initially. And didn't maybe think about it a whole lot after that. It stuck with me for a while and then after the war and everything else, those thoughts sort of go away. But I started listening to the radio as I got older and into high school and the music.

RON JACOBS: Okay, just a second. So, what you're saying is the notch of awareness of what radio could do was cranked up when FDR dies. But, from then on you knew that it could deliver more than just words. It wasn't any big deal until you got interested in music?

BILL DRAKE: The thing is, my interest in life changed because then, you know, when you get to be a teenager you start getting interested in girls and listening to music and you're thirteen, fourteen. That was five, six years after Roosevelt died.

Father Figures

RON JACOBS: What's the first thing you remember in Donalsonville? At what age? 'Cause I can't remember much about anything at a really young age.

BILL DRAKE: Well, before my father went into the Army—I must have been what, five years old at the time.

RON JACOBS: 1941, the war starts, and you and I are four years old.

BILL DRAKE: It was actually 1942 because it was at the end of 1941. And then he enlisted in mid-1942 so I was five and a half years old.

RON JACOBS: I was living seven miles from where the Japanese attacked Pearl Harbor in 1941. Do you remember when your father left to go to war?

BILL DRAKE: Um hm, I remember that, yeah.

RON JACOBS: How old do you think your father was then?

BILL DRAKE: I think he was 30. During that time, we lived with my grandfather, my mother and I. My grandparents, Mama and Papa Drake had twelve children, and they were all grown and had married and moved from home. So, when my father went in the army—it was very usual in those days that people would move in with their parents so while Daddy was in the army, we lived with Mama and Papa Drake.

RON JACOBS: And your grandfather was retired by then?

BILL DRAKE: No, he was Mayor of Iron City, Georgia and the Postmaster. And had a farm, stuff like that, and owned some property.

RON JACOBS: So that's a prestige thing, right?

BILL DRAKE: Well, it was particularly good during the war because with the Post Office thing it was a necessary thing so you had gas rations and had food.

RON JACOBS: So, for you, that must have been sort of cool if you're living with your grandpa and he's got it made. Plus, the kids are out of the house, so you're with your mother and your grandparents and both of them are alive and they're probably not all that old.

BILL DRAKE: No, well Papa Drake died when he was 98 years old, my grandmother died when she was 87 I think. My father didn't get back home until about eight months after World War II was over because he was wounded over there. And so, he spent a lot of time in hospitals after the trip back over here. And the war ended in 1945 so it was 1946 before he got home. And he was back here but he was in hospitals. They had to give him two steel hips and half a diaphragm.

RON JACOBS: Jesus! From some horrible infantry thing or what?

BILL DRAKE: Well, it was shrapnel.

RON JACOBS: In Europe?

BILL DRAKE: He eventually wound up in those days—they can do wonders today—in those days that would put the steel things in and it worked. He could operate all right for like maybe about five years.

RON JACOBS: Operate?

BILL DRAKE: I mean he could function.

RON JACOBS: Did this happen in Europe or in the Pacific?

BILL DRAKE: It was in France and Italy.

RON JACOBS: When the shit was hitting the fan.

BILL DRAKE: Uh huh.

RON JACOBS: Jesus! So, he got purple hearts and stuff?

BILL DRAKE: Oh, he got more than that.

RON JACOBS: So, tell me.

BILL DRAKE: No, no, I don't know a lot about medals, not familiar with that, but I know that he had half a diaphragm—

RON JACOBS: Well, I'm not talking about the physical part—

BILL DRAKE: —one lung, half a diaphragm, cut from here to here (pointing to his midsection). Steel things to replace his hips. And those things in those days didn't last too long so eventually happened was that his legs wouldn't function.

RON JACOBS: How did you deal with that emotionally?

BILL DRAKE: Well, I dealt with it. I figured if he could deal with it I could deal with it.

RON JACOBS: So, in a way that was probably character building.

BILL DRAKE: No, I wouldn't say it was character builder.

RON JACOBS: For you?

BILL DRAKE: No, it's basically a natural thing. I knew that it was bad and I knew that he would prefer that it hadn't happened, but it had and he was dealing with it as best he could. And if he could deal with it then sure as hell I could. It was him that was hurting, you know.

RON JACOBS: I know but to me looking at it, journalistically or whatever, it sounds like character builder to me because we all have within us some Freudian thing for or against our father.

BILL DRAKE: Oh, that was a pretty natural thing I think, at the time. It was part of the mood of the whole country. People were like that back then, in the South. I mean I don't know about you 'coconut boys' over there in Hawaii. (Laughs).

RON JACOBS: I'm just saying had your father—I don't want to belabor this—but had your father gone to the war, nothing happens to him, OK, everything happens normal. But, your father comes back with this terrifying physical stuff which doesn't just wing him in the shoulder or whatever. Goes through the rehab which is nothing compared to today, and so you're not just a guy seeing your father come back, you're seeing a guy go through a lot of stuff and you're saying if he can do it I can do it. And I think that's character building.

BILL DRAKE: I don't know if it was even that or not because you have to realize I didn't see my dad's point. And when he came back I didn't see him right away. Neither did the family. My mother went down there. He was at a Veteran's Hospital in Florida.

RON JACOBS: But you were aware when he finally showed up.

BILL DRAKE: Yeah, but you don't see that. When he did get back they had him pretty well pieced back together. And he didn't complain—

RON JACOBS: That's what I'm saying!

BILL DRAKE: —and so I figured that was cool and of course when that happened you know, with him later eventually those things, those steel things they put in started wearing out the bone.

RON JACOBS: I don't know, it seems to me—because I can't think of a time—and of course you and I have professionally known each other. But I've never seen you come close to blowing your cool. And I think that that is maybe where that starts, I don't know.

And then also if you want to talk about genetically, you talk about a grandfather that's such a respected person and you're growing up. Probably when you were living with your grandfather, you realized you couldn't even try to get away with anything.

BILL DRAKE: Oh, I tried.

RON JACOBS: Like, what's the worst that you did?

BILL DRAKE: That he did to me?

RON JACOBS: Well, let's start with what's the first thing you did?

BILL DRAKE: Oh. Well, first of all—.

RON JACOBS: Now we get to the good shit.

BILL DRAKE: I must have been—God, I think it had to have been before my father went back from the army—he used to smoke cigars and pipe and also chewed tobacco.

RON JACOBS: Jesus.

BILL DRAKE: Well, everybody did down there. But I remember when I was a kid I stole one of his cigars and it's a large house. I went back to see it later. It didn't seem nearly as large now but it seemed very large then. So, at the far end of the house there was another fireplace and chimney so I'd go underneath the house and get behind that chimney with the cigars that I had stolen. Well, I 'm back there puffing on this son of a bitch—

RON JACOBS: Did you get sick to your stomach?

BILL DRAKE: No. Well, I'd just started. And all of a sudden I hear "PHILLIP BOY"!

RON JACOBS: That's what he called you, PHILLIP BOY?

BILL DRAKE: No, he just called me PHILLIP and when he was pissed he called me PHILLIP BOY. So, this was PHILLIP BOY. I knew this was bad. 'Cause he could see the smoke coming into the house, like the goddamn place was on fire.

RON JACOBS: Wasn't he the fire chief too?

BILL DRAKE: No, he wasn't. We didn't even have a fire department then. But he hauled me into the house and said, "You've been smoking out there haven't you?"

"Yes sir."

"So, you want to smoke."

"Uh huh."

Now I wished at that point in time that he'd beat the hell out of me, which he didn't.

He said, "Well, come on with me."

So he had a big screen porch about half as big as this bar and sat me down in the chair opposite him. Lit another cigar. He lit one up, said "You want to smoke? Go ahead."

Well, he made me smoke that cigar, I got so goddamn sick I wished he'd beat the hell out of me at that point.

RON JACOBS: Now this we call a character builder.

BILL DRAKE: I got so sick.

RON JACOBS: So, it seems to me then at a time when it's all formative that you really benefited from being around your grandfather.

BILL DRAKE: Oh, absolutely. I mean I used to totally try to impress him that I knew what was going on. I remember he had cotton fields and he had onion fields and he had different vegetables and this, that and the other, and one thing that he used to like to quote even when I was out here and would go back when he was still alive—

RON JACOBS: And he lived to?

BILL DRAKE: 98 years old.

RON JACOBS: What year, do you know?

BILL DRAKE: I can't remember. But at any rate, he used to love to tell the story of when I was a kid that I would walk around behind him like this and—

RON JACOBS: With your hands on your hips?

BILL DRAKE: Because he'd be out talking to the people and he would do this, that and the other, and I would say, "Oh, Papa Drake, this cotton soon's going to be big enough to eat!" (Laughs.)

I didn't even know what the hell they did with cotton! He used to love to tell that story. And he used to say, "How bright can you be, PHILLIP!"

Paying Dues

RON JACOBS: So, after years of paying your dues in small market radio around Georgia, you end up at last in Atlanta on WAKE.

BILL DRAKE: From 1958 to 1961. First the all-night show, then I went to midday, then I went to midday and afternoon drive and production director.

RON JACOBS: I've done that, too.

BILL DRAKE: The owner of WAKE would have these old buddies of his and he'd go out and they'd sell him these things and as a special favor to them, he'd do their commercials personally. This guy never heard of a 60 second commercial. You'd give the time away. I told him nobody wants to hear this. And that's when I said to him: If anybody ever put on a radio station that was designed for the audience and not for the advertisers, the world would be a better place.

RON JACOBS: That's a great quote.

BILL DRAKE: Oh yeah. Because I'm thinking who on God's earth will listen to that? That was my theory.

RON JACOBS: But, both of us had to pay our dues in the radio business.

BILL DRAKE: We sure did.

RON JACOBS: I mean because both of us, before we were 20 or 21, had already done everything there was. Because when I did the all night—

BILL DRAKE: From sleeping at the radio station to—

RON JACOBS: You got it.

BILL DRAKE: To clearing the teletype machine—

RON JACOBS: You got it, you got it!

BILL DRAKE: To writing commercials, to helping write the logs.

RON JACOBS: Right. So, the station management has no idea what they're asking us to do. The way I started learning radio, I dropped out of school the minute I heard there was an all-night gig. I ran in there and got three bucks an hour. But I'd put on the longest track—that's why I remember Montovani–and while that record was playing on the air, screw it, I'd let it track and I'd go through and I'd read everything in every desk drawer that wasn't locked. I mean that was my way of like learning and stuff like that. And shoot, I mean in those days we would do anything to learn whatever we could learn.

BILL DRAKE: It never occurred to me not to do that. I mean I wanted to, and I wanted to learn. The teletype machine or even learning how it worked or writing commercials or anything.

RON JACOBS: Right, I would go into a station on a Sunday and see fricking teletype piling up in the "newsroom," that's been sitting there for a day and a half. I mean what kind of idiots are these guys? Not professional people. And we had to learn to read news and to be able to pronounce words correctly.

First Radio Job at 93 on the Dial

BILL DRAKE: My basketball coach was a guy who had been a basketball star at the University of Georgia. His first coaching job was at Seminole County High School. Of course, he wasn't making a whole lot of money so he had a roommate and lived in this young men's boarding house. His roommate at that time was doing a show out of Donalsonville that he had done by telephone line to the Bainbridge radio station. Donalsonville didn't have a radio station. It was done over a telephone line and he had a show called "Breakfast with Bill" every morning. The owner of the station wanted to do a thing in Bainbridge but he also figured if he could get a local thing out of Donalsonville which was closer, it's 20 miles away, that he could get commercials out of there. So, Bill Fowler was doing two hours a day out of Donalsonville.

RON JACOBS: Over a telephone line.

BILL DRAKE: Yeah, and playing records, too, down that line. Had a little studio. And as a matter of fact, the studio was put in what used to be the old People's Theater, the movie theater which closed down. And the studio itself was actually put in the ticket booth! Yeah.

RON JACOBS: Cool-looking thing, huh?

BILL DRAKE: Yeah, well, you know.

RON JACOBS: This was your start on the air?

BILL DRAKE: Yeah. And so, a friend of mine named Jack Hall, who was in my high school class, he knew Bill Fowler.

RON JACOBS: Who was older.

BILL DRAKE: Yeah. Well, he at that time was what, 24, 25.

RON JACOBS: Which in those days seemed real old.

BILL DRAKE: Yeah. I was a sophomore in high school. So, they wanted to do a weekly teen-oriented disk jockey thing to fill FCC commitments at the station for education. So, Bill Fowler had asked Jack Hall if he wanted to do the show. Jack didn't want to, so I eventually said, "Hell, I'll do it."

RON JACOBS: Was it sort of exciting?

BILL DRAKE: Yeah, I thought hey, I'd like to do that. I remember that I liked the music so I figured that'd be good. And it was called Teen Time.

RON JACOBS: Sorry, mine was called Teen Town.

BILL DRAKE: Well, la di dah!

RON JACOBS: See, it's amazing because I did Teen Town Topics and you did—.

BILL DRAKE: Teen Time. Came out of this Donalsonville studio at the former movie theater. The rest had been closed off.

All the seats were still there but they were all sealed off. A backfire out front in the street would shake the whole goddamn building.

RON JACOBS: So, you were doing this by yourself? Spinning records out of nowhere?

BILL DRAKE: I remember the first time I was on the radio, I had everything laid out. And the first song that I played on the radio was *Unchained Melody* by Roy Hamilton. And there were three versions—that's the only time that three versions of the same song were in the top five at the same time. There Les Baxter, Al Hibbler, and Roy Hamilton.

RON JACOBS: Why did you choose the Hamilton version?

BILL DRAKE: 'Cause that's the only one we had! (Laughs)

RON JACOBS: OK. No, because the Baxter version was the big orchestration and the Hibbler version was the soul one. But, there's nothing the matter with the one that you played. And that was by then, a 45.

BILL DRAKE: A 45, yeah.

RON JACOBS: OK, so were people looking at you from the street?

BILL DRAKE: Yeah! They had things in there—

RON JACOBS: Loudspeakers?

BILL DRAKE: Well, no—you have to realize Donalsonville is a very small town.

RON JACOBS: But, I mean could they hear you out on the street?

BILL DRAKE: I really can't remember. I'm sure we probably had little speakers out there.

RON JACOBS: And you had blind faith that somehow your voice and the record was going down some telephone wire and going into where the transmitter was at?

BILL DRAKE: The telephone line went to the Bainbridge studio and they took that and sent it up to the transmitter. But by the way, the station was at 930 on the dial. Like KHJ.

RON JACOBS: And what were the call letters?

BILL DRAKE: (Sings to the tune of the KHJ jingles) 93, WMGR! (Laughs.)

RON JACOBS: When are we talking now, Bill? What year are you in school?

BILL DRAKE: Well, "Unchained Melody" had been, what, 1954.

RON JACOBS: So, were you like a junior in high school?

BILL DRAKE: I guess so, yeah.

RON JACOBS: So, it's 1954 and was it before or after the basketball season?

BILL DRAKE: I don't remember.

RON JACOBS: But wait a second. *Unchained Melody* was the number one song at that time, right?

BILL DRAKE: Yeah. Well, of the three versions that were in the top five, I don't which was number one, but I'm saying Roy Hamilton's version was the only one that we had so I liked that song and I played it.

RON JACOBS: For me to pin this down accurately, I'm going to come in and say that the first record you played in the box office of the People's Theater was *Unchained Melody*. Like, I happen to remember the exact day I got my FCC license because it was Christmas Eve, 1952.

BILL DRAKE: I don't know. What happened was: I had everything pretty well laid out, trying to plan and I got everything ready. And I remember starting *Unchained Melody* by Roy Hamilton. The record was supposed to be 2:05 or 2:20. And all I remember was that sucker couldn't have been more than 3 seconds long because when it ended I was not ready.

RON JACOBS: And, thus, the Drake Format is born! (Drake laughs.) In 1954. And this is why years later, some 7,000 disc jockeys have had the shit beaten into them: BE READY!! Right?

BILL DRAKE: It was just over! And I was not ready.

Before Boss Radio

RON JACOBS: Over you career, you've been on the air, yourself, and you've been a program director. How do you feel about radio personalities?

BILL DRAKE: You know, I've always had a problem with people saying that they're personalities in radio. I've known a few. Robert W. Morgan was a personality. The Real Don Steele was a personality; Steele didn't talk too much, but he had a personality.

Bob McKee was a personality, a guy on Atlanta radio. The thing is he talked too fucking much.

RON JACOBS: But we didn't have role models. The radio business, I mean. We were all inventing shit as we went along.

BILL DRAKE: But the thing is of course, personalities, you can look at some of the greatest jocks of all time as far as people remember, they'll tell you Morgan, Steele, Charlie Tuna. Maybe it's the name, I don't know. I can tell you one thing about that. When you think about it, it's interesting. We were involved in a great window of opportunity, a great thing, a combination of me, you, them, the time, everything else. When I used to be on the air, no, I was not a personality. I didn't tell jokes, I didn't play wild tracks—.

San Francisco

BILL DRAKE: I got to KYA in San Francisco in 1961 and turned it around [in the radio ratings].

RON JACOBS: Were you on the air and also program director?

BILL DRAKE: Uh huh.

RON JACOBS: So, who was doing morning drive?

BILL DRAKE: I was.

RON JACOBS: Really! And being PD.

BILL DRAKE: Yep.

RON JACOBS: Was there a group name for the KYA jocks? I've seen pictures of you and those guys wearing coats and stuff.

BILL DRAKE: No. But I think one thing that probably has gone unnoticed is Clancy Imuslind.

RON JACOBS: Clancy was who came up with what?

BILL DRAKE: The phrase. At KYA. "The Boss of the Bay".

RON JACOBS: That wasn't your line?

BILL DRAKE: Clancy's. And in 1965 at KHJ, you didn't like the phrase "Boss Radio"—neither did I. But, I said alright because KYA was "The Boss of the Bay."

RON JACOBS: It's just so weird.

BILL DRAKE: All I know is I thought that you came up with it.

RON JACOBS: No! Clancy came up with it. So, the first manifestation of the Drake Format happened at KYA when you got there.

BILL DRAKE: Oh yeah.

RON JACOBS: There are stories people tell of how Clint Churchill was the owner KYA and he comes in and tells you "You're out in one day." But, the fact that you put up with Churchill for a whole year is great.

BILL DRAKE: Clint Churchill could not handle Tom Donahue, who drove him unmercifully. And you know, Clint had it and he wanted me to fire Donahue.

RON JACOBS: Probably one of the three greatest disk jockeys in America at that time.

BILL DRAKE: And I said—obviously, I didn't like the little son of a bitch Churchill anyhow—but I dealt with it. I said "You want him fired, you fire him. I'm not going to do it." And I said, "I'm leaving."

RON JACOBS: You said, "Do it and I'm leaving"?

BILL DRAKE: I said, "You do it, I'm leaving." I said "I'll tell you what, Clint. I'll bet you anything you want to bet that when the new [ratings] book comes out Donahue will have the highest goddamn ratings on the radio station."

RON JACOBS: So, you're trying to tell me that the guy calls you in to get rid of one of the best jocks in the country and certainly the best that's maybe ever been seen in San Francisco, and he ends up losing you. And then your prediction comes true about Donahue's ratings being the highest, and then Donahue splits because he can't take Churchill anymore.

BILL DRAKE: That's a natural fact. That was the reason that I got more joy out of later with programming KFRC. We destroyed KYA in like six months with KFRC.

Fresno

RON JACOBS: When was the first time that you met Gene Chenault?

BILL DRAKE: In Fresno.

RON JACOBS: What I want to know is, since your life had been in San Francisco, what did you know of the scene in Fresno?

BILL DRAKE: I knew nothing.

RON JACOBS: I mean you didn't know that Chenault had been number one in the ratings with KYNO?

BILL DRAKE: Oh, I knew that, yeah, but I'd never heard the radio station. Chenault told me that he'd gotten his ass kicked.

RON JACOBS: And he says right off, honestly, "I need help"?

BILL DRAKE: Uh huh. I listened to the radio and I looked at him and I said "Gene, you're in fucking trouble!" (Laughs.)

RON JACOBS: If I were writing this or if we were videoing this, I must make note that in these first references, Mr. Drake has been making horrible facial expressions to go along with what he's been saying about his opinions of KYNO at the time. But did you line it out to Chenault in order, like too many commercials, not enough this or just said totally just fucked?

BILL DRAKE: I didn't tell him a whole lot about anything. I told him that he was in trouble and I said this radio station is–.

RON JACOBS: "This" being?

BILL DRAKE: K-MAK. Where you were PD.

RON JACOBS: When you drove into Fresno, did you think at that time that K-MAK was an LA-level station even at that point? Or not because we didn't get better until we started competing with you?

BILL DRAKE: I wasn't thinking about that at the time.

RON JACOBS: Can you remember the first time you and I actually saw each other? 'Cause I can.

BILL DRAKE: The first time I remember was at the Fresno County Fair.

RON JACOBS: Right, right.

BILL DRAKE: I remember somebody said "That's Jacobs over there." (Laughs.)

RON JACOBS: Right, right, right.

BILL DRAKE: And you were going like "Hmm."

RON JACOBS: That was really great man, because there was a respect thing, you know.

BILL DRAKE: I said before now, many times before, that either of those radio stations at that time in 1963 could have walked into LA. The thing that really occurred was, as far as a program director, I knew that you were the best I'd ever come up against, and you're still the best I've ever seen.

RON JACOBS: Thanks, man.

Rockumentary: The History of Rock and Roll

RON JACOBS: When we finished the last 24 hours of "The History of Rock and Roll" in 1969, it was insane. Pete Johnson was crawling on the floor, Robert W. Morgan was about to pass out, Bill Mouzis let me run the board. I'm freaking out because I know [some major event such as] Harry Truman is doing to die within four minutes of when it's supposed to go on. A guy had stolen my radio that I had planned to listen to it on. And then it was over. My phone didn't ring. And I thought we had laid the biggest egg in the history of radio. Now you had a blast going on in your house or something when it was on?

BILL DRAKE: Probably. I don't remember.

RON JACOBS: OK, but what was your feeling? Because you guys had come down–. Someone at KHJ had asked for a sales demo when we had about 4 hours together. We squeezed it together and the first time you and Gene Chenault came down, we just smashed together 3 or so hours.

BILL DRAKE: The main problem that I remember that we had to deal with was: I wanted to go what—at that time it was 48 hours I think and later it was 52 hours. But in doing that, I remember in designing it, we had to plan so that the weaker stuff showed up like in the all-night show. And we found out later people were sitting up all night listening and taping the thing.

RON JACOBS: Yeah, and also what was the weaker stuff from a standard top 40 standpoint allowed me, in the only time I was there, and the only time that I was able to do it, and you didn't hassle me, I was able to do my far-out things. Like interview Phil Spector, which was a classic, for 15 minutes, which he would never do. Steve Allen comes in and he reads the lyrics to songs. We had the Bob Dylan stuff, you know. We had these things in the middle of the night that we called prime sweep and stuff like that, that now people—that was like ten, twenty years ahead of its time. But, what I'm trying to figure out as you were hearing it—like when I heard it–it was like you paint the Golden Gate bridge and you go back from where you started. When you were hearing it, when you heard it, when I heard it, it was like I was hearing shit that I couldn't even remember because we had produced it 2 months before. When you were hearing it, you were hearing it more like watching a movie for the first time. So, did it just blow you away, just keep coming at you or what?

BILL DRAKE: Oh yeah, but you have to realize, I was pretty well up on things anyhow. I knew what to expect. And as far as the design and so forth, the layout of what we had to have. And here again, it was just so different at the time. It wasn't brain surgery, it was a lot of work.

RON JACOBS: Did you stay up and hear any of the offbeat stuff?

BILL DRAKE: I don't remember.

RON JACOBS: But I think that I had heard that when it was over, which was at noon, that you had some people there and you had an idea it was a pretty big deal. I got nothing until—. I thought we had bombed. No phone calls. And then I go in the next day and there's people with telegrams saying, "I was on my way to New York and I got sucked in and I stayed overnight at a motel listening to it," and Dick Clark is sending in all this stuff and all the yadda

yadda that happened after it. And it went on to become what it went on to become.

BILL DRAKE: Well, it was the first of those things that was ever done.

RON JACOBS: Rockumentary.

After Boss Radio

RON JACOBS: At KHJ, the deal was pretty cool in that we had set it up so if you had any problem you would talk to me and so the jocks wouldn't be getting it from two different directions and mixed signals and shit.

BILL DRAKE: I thought that was the most important thing. And I had worked what was before. I'd seen the horrors of what can happen and of course the general manager was kept out of that, you know, it was the program director. And it was the first time I think, that programmers really ran radio stations. General managers could run the overall station, they could run sales, Sales managers could run sales, but I always thought a programmer should program, sales people should sell, and, if I got in the middle of that—if you had been at KHJ and I had been going around you and behind your back all the time saying that, that and the other and so forth, that's the reason. Good God, you know, even when we brought Bill Watson in, he would call you. Or I would call you. But, it had to be a thing that those jocks had to know that if they screwed with Ron Jacobs, they were going to be fucked. And they couldn't go around us and it couldn't be allowed.

RON JACOBS: I mean no internal shit never got leaked out of there. The thing is, I think in the beginning man, you and I were talking to each other a lot.

BILL DRAKE: Oh, yeah, absolutely. On a constant basis.

About the Music

RON JACOBS: So, about the music, I would only deal with it after [music director] Betty Brenneman had gone through it. And what were you doing, you were giving Betty ideas too?

BILL DRAKE: Well, yeah, there was a thing of—it was filtered in a few things… I mean she would deal with the record people or you or whoever would—.

RON JACOBS: I never talked to them. But you were actually taking the time to listen to full records.

BILL DRAKE: Oh yeah. And we had to—I thought I was doing it for the other stations like KGB and KYNO here and then later with others. But it was a thing of overall, everything was filtered through Betty even from the other stations. See, I had to deal with the other stations too on that basis. And the good thing was that I could take these ideas and could break them down to simplistic things that the guy working at the service station or

McDonald's or whatever could do. And remember I used to say, "This is not radio man's radio."

RON JACOBS: Yeah, but the best thing we had going man, was that I'm too far out and you want to take it back out and the place where we met in the middle was always cool.

BILL DRAKE: That's why it worked.

RON JACOBS: Because the music that you were listening to at home was different from the music that I was listening to at home. I'm at home listening to Miles Davis, right? But it had nothing to do with work.

BILL DRAKE: Well, I realized we couldn't make a living on KHJ with Miles Davis.

RON JACOBS: More into Phil Spector's works.

BILL DRAKE: Greatest producer I ever knew.

RON JACOBS: And that section in "The History of Rock and Roll" I did in 1969, I didn't believe Spector was ever going to go for that, that he actually came out and did that. Because that was based on the old jazz magazine blindfold test deal. And he really got into it.

BILL DRAKE: The thing is, he liked KHJ a lot.

RON JACOBS: Oh yeah?

BILL DRAKE: Yeah. I remember the first time I met Spector, we were at Martoni's one night and the place was packed. And the bar, the people were like three of four deep. I'm 6'6" and he's not. This was before The Byrds and the granny glasses and all this.

Spector's there, he's go on this leather jacket, got his goatee. He's got on some kind of leather hat.

RON JACOBS: And he's like twenty years old.

BILL DRAKE: Yeah, and he's got all this shit on, and these granny glasses, and he's got on these motorcycle boots, this, that and the other. And he and I are trying to talk like this close in a crowded bar. And I'm thinking to myself, "This is the strangest looking guy I have ever seen!" And there was a lull in the conversation and he looked at me and said, "You know, Drake," and I knew he was serious. He said, "A lot of strange looking people in here."

The Best

RON JACOBS: Putting KHJ aside, what do you think was the best RKO station of that era?

BILL DRAKE: Aside from KHJ?

RON JACOBS: Yeah, put KHJ aside because we know KHJ was—if KHJ wasn't the best one, we should just stop the tape. I mean that's a given.

BILL DRAKE: Obviously after KHJ the best was KFRC.

RON JACOBS: Because?

BILL DRAKE: Well, I think because of a lot of factors. Had a good feel. It was very close in the heels of KHJ. The problem we had with people that we'd send to San Francisco would be you'd send them up there and in three fucking months they're wearing beads and doped out and drugged out and sitting on the goddamn corner and chanting and marching in parades. I mean that really happened.

RON JACOBS: Best non-RKO station, or, the best station that you didn't have anything to do with.

BILL DRAKE: I can't think of any.

RON JACOBS: Oh, come on.

BILL DRAKE: Ah.... different time, different situation, and of course a lot of it had to do with signals. You have to realize that poor timing. WLS in Chicago was a good station at the time because it was playing 30 records.

RON JACOBS: What time period?

BILL DRAKE: You're talking late 1950s. Early 1960s. And WABC in New York. They had 50,000 watts.

RON JACOBS: Let's talk about music. For the whole time, who was the best male artist?

BILL DRAKE: Oh good God, that's—.

RON JACOBS: A hard one, eh? But, I mean Elvis has to be in there, right?

BILL DRAKE: Well, yeah, but there's no way you can go into that. You have to realize that most of the time that we were at KHJ, Elvis's records sucked. I used to talk to Elvis about it. And the thing is, that was because of Colonel Tom Parker saying—these godawful movies are what made money. But, for his records, Elvis hadn't had a fucking hit in years because of that. Elvis got on the phone one time and said, "Damn, Drake, I had more hit records before I met you." And I said, "Elvis, you recorded more hit records before you met me!" (Laughs.)

RON JACOBS: OK, when did you first meet Elvis? Before KHJ when you were in Atlanta or what?

BILL DRAKE: No, I met him in Las Vegas for the first time. I remember Elvis opened the door and I'd seen the show. But to see him up close! He was the most gorgeous son of a bitch I'd ever seen in my life. And he said, "Ah! I know you're Bill Drake!" He said, "Damn, you're even taller than they said you were."

The Mystique

RON JACOBS: So, what about underexposure and the Drake mystique? Always you don't know where the guy is, you can't get him on the phone, you gotta go through people to get to him and this just makes for a bigger mystique. What is that? I mean, did you do that deliberately? Because remember you told me you wouldn't even take Gene Chenault's phone calls when you were in San Francisco at KYA.

BILL DRAKE: Well, that's true, I don't talk to people I don't know. And I also realized that in the situation that you and I wound up in as far as when this happened, you got everybody coming at you out of the woodwork from one side or the other and you start dealing with that stuff you can't do—that's the reason I didn't want to be in radio stations all the time.

RON JACOBS: What do you mean, when "this" happened?

BILL DRAKE: When Boss Radio happened. When Los Angeles happened. The thing is, at that point what's going to happen is, you're going to have all the stuff music business, people in radio, this, that and the other, all trying to glom and you start dealing with that stuff you can't maintain what you're supposed to be doing. And no, it wasn't a design or a thing of trying to create anything at all. All I was trying to do was to avoid dealing with the bullshit so that I could concentrate on what I should be concentrating on. But there was no design, other than to keep the bullshit away from me. That's all I was trying to do.

And I guess, as it turned out, the less of that stuff I did, the more they said about it, which was certainly not my intention. But the thing is, I couldn't have dealt with every record promotion man or people in radio and this, that and the other, of being available to them or people writing—. I never in my life tried to get an article written about me. And the thing is, articles were written and sometimes I got burned in a thing like that. And you're just trying to avoid the horseshit so you can concentrate on what you're concentrating on.

No, it wasn't no design as far as trying to do anything other than keep things as calm as you can because that can gobble you up, man. People coming in writing this or record promotion men doing this and people saying this and people in the radio business saying this, that and the other. And you deal with them and you say, Good God, who needs that? I never wanted that!

RON JACOBS: It had to be a kick coming from Donalsonville, Georgia to see like an article about you in *Time* magazine, or to be in a 1971 Dewars Scotch ad in national magazines. I mean you can't tell me that that wasn't a kick, come on man.

BILL DRAKE: It sure was, particularly to my mother. Because if you remember, *Time* magazine—and this is the only thing I remember about the article—they called me "a monument to public tastelessness!" (Laughs.)

RON JACOBS: Good. Well, that I don't remember.

BILL DRAKE: And then right underneath the picture, they called me a "country bumpkin"!

RON JACOBS: Hmmm. And then the Dewars Scotch ad.

BILL DRAKE: I don't even drink Scotch.

RON JACOBS: And they didn't care?

BILL DRAKE: No. They contact people and say well, so you get publicity. That Dewars Profile thing. I don't drink Scotch. And then they said they didn't care.

What is Most Important

RON JACOBS: OK, so work is more important essentially.

BILL DRAKE: Well, Ron, it wasn't a thing of that necessarily. Work was certainly—what I was concentrating on was more important. But, I never cared about trying to stand in front of a whole lot of people that don't mean shit to me and convince them of anything at all. To me it was irrelevant. It made no difference whatsoever. It was all horseshit. They're all there for whatever their reasons are and I also know that it's usually with ulterior motives. And I found no enjoyment or possibility of enjoyment. I mean that's crap to me.

RON JACOBS: Do you think that was, in a way, the best thing you've done? I mean KHJ during those several years? I do. I mean I think that was the best thing I did—in that area. I mean making albums is another thing, syndication's another thing but as far as running a live station.

BILL DRAKE: Oh yeah. That was definitely the most fun and more lucrative things has happened to me but I think, to anybody who was involved in that—particularly you and me—it's almost sad that so many people that have been in the business or are in the business or would be in the business, very few of them will ever have that kind of thing happen to them at such a time, on such a level with such impact which is still related to very fondly by so many people in the business. You and I used to be the bitterest of "enemies"—you know, competitors.

RON JACOBS: Yeah, but that's why we respected each other.

BILL DRAKE: Of course! And that's why I said, "Hey, he's the best!" But as far as things and people, we're very lucky, Ron. Very few people ever in the business have gone through something like that. But the impact at the time, you know, very few people have had that kind of thing happen. In radio, I think we probably had one of the best. There are probably too many people that we should give credit to. I mean, we can't think about it. You can't compress 35 or 40 years into a thing of sitting down and talking about something in that amount of time. I'm sure a lot of people are well deserving that contributed to me and to you, and the whole phenomenon that happened that frankly at the time we had no idea who. We were too goddamn busy doing what we were doing; we had no idea what was going on out there. And I'm sure people were overlooked.

RON JACOBS: What do you think is the overall biggest misconception if you want to talk about the Drake Format–the whole generic thing. That's it and that's what it's going to go down as. What do you think is the biggest misconception?

BILL DRAKE: I have no idea what the biggest is. There are a lot of misconceptions, and I think probably the only people that know about that would be people like you and me who were there at the time. And you'll have all kinds of people that had all kinds of opinions and this, that and the other. They weren't there, they don't know, and probably have a preconceived idea going in. So as far as misconceptions, who knows, but there were a lot of them and some were accurate You can't tell about misconceptions, you know.

RON JACOBS: And also, it happened at what was maybe the most exciting time in American popular music.

BILL DRAKE: Can you imagine if we'd started KHJ in the John Denver era? We'd have been fucked.

Physical Remnants

A broadcasting tower located in the Fairfax District of Los Angeles transmitted the KHJ radio signal for several decades. It was torn down in 2013 to make room for more Los Angeles paved streets, sidewalks, and residences.

The former location of the KHJ radio and television studios and offices remains a popular culture landmark in Hollywood. You can walk or drive by on Melrose Avenue adjacent to Paramount Pictures and across the street from Lucy's El Adobe Cafe.

Don't Know Much About History

That famous radio documentary in 1969 that originally was produced for broadcast in Los Angeles on KHJ remained a core source of anger for Jacobs directed towards the Drake-Chenault team. But, I never saw any evidence whatsoever that Jacobs held onto anger specifically or personally against Drake about what happened concerning "The History of Rock and Roll."

During the 1970s, the Drake-Chenault radio programming and syndication company crafted a derivative and updated 52-hour adaptation of the original 1969 documentary that was distributed on tape on a syndicated basis to other radio stations. Nobody should mistake that syndicated Drake-Chenault version with the first and original version from 1969 created by Jacobs and narrated by Robert W. Morgan for broadcast on KHJ.

There is one crucial account about "The History of Rock and Roll" that I share with you here in this book: Ellen Pelissero was employed at KHJ in the mid-1960s. She worked on the first and original version that was broadcast on KHJ in 1969. She of all people certainly would know the honest truth about what happened. What she has to say clears away many decades of doubt over who did what, when and where. In her own words that were first posted on www.bossradioforever.com, here is how Ellen

Pelissero remembers the creation and production of that original radio documentary:

While Bill Mouzis and I busted *okole* on the syndicated version of The History of Rock and Roll (HRR)—for which he received $500 and I was offered a $5 a week raise—the origination of the idea for HRR came from a KHJ sales presentation film (which became an RKO radio sales film) that I wrote and produced (in its entirety) as a sort of "mini history of rock and roll" with the purpose of acquainting then middle-aged women media buyers with the vitality of the AM rock 'n' roll radio station market. It was called "The Beat Goes On."

With me on that project were Bill Mouzis engineering and directing and Bob Morgan lending his incredible voice and talent to the mix. (My main "extra" in the film—the man in the couple enjoying this KHJ music—was, incidentally my then next door neighbor, Don Imus.)

With a guy in the sales staff (whose name escapes me now, but he was blond) and Ed DelaPeña from engineering, I flew up to San Francisco for the KHJ/RKO sales presentation. Bill Drake was at that sales presentation and actually spoke to me about it; complimenting me on the work. As I said, from there it went on to be the RKO Radio chain's sales presentation (I still have the audio track but not the film itself. I think Bill Mouzis had a copy.

Now clearly our work wasn't the entire kernel for HRR, but it was certainly a part of it, because shortly after that sales film Ron hired me out of the traffic/sales department to work with him, Pete Johnson, Bill Mouzis and Bob Morgan and Sandy (Mandelbaum) Gibson on the project. And in the 13 or so weeks of production, the ONLY other persons at KHJ, RKO or Drake/Chenault that had anything whatsoever to do with the production were our music director and Shelley (Gordon) Morgan who spent a lot of time holding us together—especially in the last weeks of production when we weren't even stopping to eat.

And our leader and coach and push-meister and inspiration and through every second of that production was the incredibly talented—albeit sometimes rough to be around—Ron Jacobs.

After a careful reading of Pelissero's explanation, there can be no doubt whatsoever in anyone's mind that Jacobs was the one who made "The History of Rock and Roll" happen in 1969. Later on, derivative versions of the documentary were produced without Jacobs by Drake-Chenault personnel and those were syndicated for broadcast on many radio stations spanning many years. If you browse the many, extensive online commentaries by Jacobs on the subject of his work at KHJ, you will find a great and enduring pride in what he accomplished in Los Angeles so long ago with this game-changing radio documentary broadcast on KHJ. You will also easily find many clear expressions of his anger following what he perceived as "getting screwed" by the Drake-Chenault company.

Chapter 16:
Adventure Repeating Itself

And, in the end, I get back to where I started: It's all about *the quest for adventure*.

I learned from The Real Don Steele that you certainly can choose to live your life and not merely exist through it. Gene Chenault is one who is remembered by his loved ones has having lived an adventurous life. Why not you, too?

In my humble opinion, you should learn to take risks in your life. You should "represent" that you are someone who knows what life is for. Hint: *It is meant to be lived*. It hold excitement that you can discover in people and places and events. You never really know what you might find. You never know what you might give back to the world.

Anyone who chooses (as I did) to work in major market broadcasting should expect interpersonal challenges. Without doubt, that industry attracts people who are unrelentingly driven to perform professionally at the highest levels. In addition, their perfectionism and drive often leads to the creation and nurturing of egos the size of the state of Alaska. So, if you are someone who wants safe and soothing interpersonal relationships, you likely will be horribly disappointed greatly by choosing to work in major market radio or television broadcasting!

I never imagined that my interest in researching and writing about the history of radio station KHJ, Los Angeles would result in me writing this book. But, I am very pleased that I could share my quest-for-adventure-story stemming from KHJ here with you as I have in this book.

If you are a young, and you are considering a career in media, there are several lessons that can be drawn from my experiences in Hollywood rock and roll radio:

Should you expect to have a similar career like the men that I have described here? Probably not.

Given the economic realities of today, you may not find a career path to being on the air talent on a radio station on a full-time basis. A major media corporation, Clear Channel, attracted negative buzz in the 21st century for firing hundreds of the company's on-air employees from across the nation to cut operating costs. But, Clear Channel is not the only media company to do so. If the past predicts the future, anyone who seeks a full-time career on the air in the radio broadcasting business in the United States today will likely have a very difficult and challenging life. Commercial broadcasting is risky business. Don't forget that.

Additionally, in the present day, we all may have to become comfortable with unhappy endings for us humans brought on by computerized technology. Writers of science fiction stories along with movie and television producers/directors have time and again warned us that we human beings just may not be sufficiently smart to save ourselves from the machines that we created.

One recent development in radio broadcasting only seems like you saw it already in a James Cameron movie. It may be nothing at all, or, this could be the proverbial handwriting on the wall that your parents always warned you to be ready to see for your own damn good: When I first started writing this book, I found a news story online about the use of computer-generated voices in United States broadcasting that suggested there just might not be a long-term need for human beings as employees to work as announcers on the air. One other example: In Las Vegas, I have been very impressed with the high level of customer service from Cox Communications that is available over the telephone. Inbound calls reach a computer-generated voice that sounds unusually genuine and, dare I say, "human."

There are many other business organizations in the second decade of the 21st century that use computer-generated human voices. Such a development probably is one more step towards manmade artificial intelligence (AI) that may ultimately emerge as a threat to our species. This is not merely about whether you will be able to get a paying gig as a radio announcer. You probably should rent Ronald D. Moore's *Battlestar Galactica* and spinoffs (2003 – 2012) because taken together, they contain what I consider to be priceless knowledge about how our human species needs to be very careful about how far we should dare trust our beloved computerized devices.

I have had many years to think about this question: Is it possible in the present day for a radio programming format as innovative and influential as was Boss Radio in 1965 in Los Angeles at RKO Radio to be developed and launched?

The short answer is: **No**.

Let me explain: It is arrogant and presumptuous to believe that the 1960s were such a singularly unique time that what came of that era culturally, politically, etc. could never happen again. Yet, to me, it seems sensible to believe that many things that grew out of the 1960s would be very difficult—if not impossible—to emulate or recreate in the present day within our present culture. This is true especially because the ways in which the entertainment and information industries in the United States do business nowadays differ substantially from how things were done during the 1960s. At the very least, the federal laws are very different today compared to 50 years ago governing what companies can or cannot do with radio stations.

Consider whether there are there any media corporations today that would dare to give any major market radio station programmers the freedom to use strategies and tactics like what made KHJ financially successful starting in 1965.

Consider whether there are any on-air personalities in any radio market today—especially in this era of mass terminations of on-air radio station employees—who can ever hope to achieve the national status and influence like Robert W. Morgan and The Real Don Steele.

There are, of course, a couple of exceptions that may provide you with some level of comfort as you consider your options at the beginning of your professional career: If you are interested in being on the air on the radio involved in talk radio or all-news radio or all-sports radio or faith programming, your prospects for employment are actually quite good. This is true because computers do not (yet) have the capability to go out on their own and interview people and edit the finished product for sharing on the air. Maybe later in this century that kind of thing may become an everyday reality. Meanwhile, the talk radio formats and the all-news radio and all-sports radio formats and faith broadcasting stations in the United States will continue to demand qualified and educated on-air personnel who breathe oxygen.

No matter what particular career path you choose, I believe that you must have your own personalized version of a quest for adventure. You should never hold yourself back from a career path in today's media. And, don't let anybody else hold you back, either.

In addition to the radio or television formats I have mentioned, you also have numerous other channels of worldwide outreach at your very fingertips. If you somehow could transport yourself back in time to interact with people in Los Angeles in 1965, consider how shocked they would be when they saw your smartphone! To the people of the 1960s, what you can do with a small hand-held device like an iPhone or Android would dazzle them as wild science fiction.

If you are clever and inventive, you can find existing digital channels right now (likely with accompanying apps for iPhone and Android) that will give you a way to make a living. Plus, if you are a content provider, you can take the digital media path and avoid all the heavy capital expenses associated with radio or television broadcasting media hardware and infrastructure. One example of this kind of success in digital distribution of oneself is Todrick Hall. This talented young man created an online following and revenue streams for himself starting on YouTube. He ended up with a leading role on Broadway in *Kinky Boots* fueling speculation that his autobiographical *Straight Outta Oz* show, which I saw in Las Vegas in 2017, will someday become a fully-produced musical.

There's no telling what further advances in hand-held technology might become available in the years ahead. But, I do know one thing: You need to prepare yourself intellectually and emotionally for whatever comes.

I strongly recommend that you select a broad communications-related major for which you can feel passion at a reputable college or university. I would also tell you from personal experience that you may not be satisfied if you earn only an undergraduate degree. You may need a graduate degree especially if you want to aim for management roles in writing, producing, and giving voice to news and sports and talk radio programming.

If news and sports and talk on radio stations somehow do not interest you professionally, then perhaps the field of public relations or marketing would be worth considering. Some journalism degree programs offer public relations as a focus, for example. Marketing degrees that prepare you for digital outreach are easy to find as well. No matter what changes you can envision happening in technology, as long as there are human beings, there will always be a need for public relations and marketing professionals. Also keep in mind that if you earn only one undergraduate degree in your life, no matter what major you select, you may nonetheless feel compelled to get a graduate degree or other supplementary training or certification if you expect to remain gainfully employable over the lifetime of your professional career.

Getting one university diploma is not to prove to anyone that you acquired wisdom. No way. Getting one university diploma mainly will prove that you could get one university diploma. Few people—especially those who work in the field of education—will be this honest with you.

I enthusiastically encourage getting a university degree or two. But, this should be attempted only by those who know another "hidden secret," so to speak: The purpose of getting a university diploma is to be in an environment where you can be trained how to use your mind. A degree from a university is certainly not for the purpose of collecting and parsing lifelong knowledge. You may or not gain any wisdom. You may or may not end up meeting people that are valuable to you over the remainder of your lifetime.

More importantly, the knowledge you may certainly collect while attending a university degree program likely will become outmoded in just a few short years after you've got your diploma anyway. Timing is everything and the passage of time can seem especially cruel.

Just as I started thinking that I had learned all I ever needed to learn—I earned an undergraduate degree and two graduate degrees before 1980—along came game-changing technology called the personal computer. That was immediately followed in the 1990s by online communities and businesses and then digital devices. I suspect that technology will likely keep changing unexpectedly and without warning.

You will see such changes in your lifetime. You would be wise to expect that you will have more than merely one professional career over your expected lifespan of 70 or 80 or 90 years. This means that what you learn during your undergraduate and graduate degree programs likely will end up being completely insufficient to serve you over your entire lifetime as you change careers in response to economic and cultural changes.

You should aim as I did for achieving the capacity to keep learning and for embracing contemporary technology no matter how many birthdays you celebrate. You should acquire life skills and the appropriate mental health to keep adapting your professional career choices to whatever happens to you in real life. I also believe that only those people who develop a genuine curiosity toward new technology (rather than a mere tolerance) will be the ones who succeed most readily with technology in the years to come.

Last, but not least, I want to discuss the important issue of the passion that you feel towards your chosen professions. My passion for radio broadcasting was unsustainable beyond one decade. That is a very short span of time. When I initially got into the radio broadcasting business, I believed subconsciously I was going to be young forever. Don't we all? And I also thought that the passion in me for the radio broadcasting business would last for many decades.

I once was someone who listened to radio at least an hour or two every day. Because I easily find many compelling alternatives today for how I get my news, weather, traffic, and music entertainment, I only listen to radio about an hour or two a month now. I'll bet that I am not the only one who would admit to such a sharp decrease in the personal use of radio.

With today's available technology, the reality is that one does not need a terrestrial broadcasting station using the radio and television frequencies at all to communicate and have an impact upon listeners around the world. I believe that the long and powerful reign of broadcast programming using over-the-air frequencies as we know them today will not survive beyond the 21st century. Even though we have made it only a mere two decades into the 21st century, just look around and you will see that there are significantly attractive and available alternatives to over-the-air broadcasts.

In your life, your mileage may vary. But, to exhaust all your passion for a chosen profession too early in life is the equivalent of running out of gas or water while driving across the Mojave Desert. If you allow me to continue this desert metaphor, let me offer a warning: Either do not cross a potentially difficult desert in your life or career, or, find ways to recharge your passions for what you do for a living.

It really all comes down to you. And, how you use your mind matters quite a bit. That's why I emphasize the need to attain and maintain mental health. Also, get a copy of *Emotional Intelligence* by Daniel Goleman and learn from the priceless wisdom it contains. You don't think that you need it. But, yes, you do need it.

Whether you're out there, shoulder-to-shoulder in the neon fun jungle, as The Real Don Steele used to say, or, someplace else doesn't really matter. I wish you the very best in your life.

This is the end of our electronic journey into the past. We now return to your life in the 21st century, already in progress.

Thank you for your interest in my writing. I wish for you the reputation of someone who shows what it means truly to be alive. That's certainly a terrific way for anyone to be perceived and remembered.

Sources Cited

The information, descriptions, claims, and quotes from people presented on this site can be attributed to a variety of sources.

The primary sources are first-person sources. These are people who were present at the time of the events they describe took place, and who either participated in the events or observed them from a very close vantage point.

Face-to-face interviews recorded on audio tape with a variety of professionals in the radio and music industries of the 1970s were conducted by me for my research during graduate school into the radio programming of Drake-Chenault on KHJ and other radio stations.

Disclaimer: The use of peoples' names in no way indicates their approval of or agreement with my commentaries or my conclusions.

I have been asked more than a couple of times about how I selected the people that I should talk to about KHJ and Drake-Chenault. Here is my answer: I relied upon the specific recommendations that were given to me by three men who were the top go-to sources at the time on the subject of KHJ and Boss Radio—Bill Gavin, Bill Drake, and Gene Chenault.

Despite some grumblings, however, this nonfiction work of mine is not an "unauthorized biography" about radio programming people or about radio stations. I have never ambushed anybody and used their comments without their knowledge. Every person, living or dead, who participated in the various telephone, in-person, and electronic mail interviews with me did so knowingly and willfully. Most importantly, nobody set any restrictions on my usage of the primary source material that I collected during my interactions with them.

Permissions were given to me by the copyright owner either verbally over the telephone or in emails so that I had the proper legal approval to reprint certain copyrighted material.

My research was published originally in my master's thesis, entitled "The Mystique and The Mass Persuasion: A Rhetorical Analysis of The Drake-Chenault Radio Programming 1965 – 1976." The document was accepted by the faculty of Humboldt State University in Arcata, CA in June 1976 in partial fulfillment of requirements for my master's degree in communications. Available free for downloading if you just Google that horrible title I chose.

Below is the complete list of the interviews and other primary source communications that serve as the origins of attributed quotes throughout this book:

Jan Basham—Hollywood, CA—December 31, 1975
Gene Chenault—Hollywood, CA—January 2, 1976
Roger Christian—Beverly Hills, CA—September 25, 1975
Mark Denis—Anaheim, CA—September 25, 1975
Ken Devaney—Fresno, CA—December 22, 1975
Bill Drake—Beverly Hills, CA—September 23, 1975
Paul Drew—Hollywood, CA—December 31, 1975
Bill Gavin—San Francisco, CA—December 19, 1975
Claude Hall—Hollywood, CA—December 30, 1975
Irving Ivers—Burbank, CA—September 23, 1975
Ron Jacobs—San Diego, CA—November 8, 1975
Bruce Johnson—Los Angeles, CA—December 26, 1975
Bert Kleiman—Hollywood, CA—December 31, 1975
Annie Van Bebber—Canoga Park, CA—September 26, 1975

I conducted additional primary research to augment and update the findings. I attained additional primary source information and quotations through my communications via electronic mail and/or telephone conversations with the following people:

Terry Corbell, 2001
Paul Drew, 2012
Clancy Imuslind, 1997
Ron Jacobs, 1997 – 2016
Hank Landsberg, 2001
Ken Levine, 1997
Gary McDowell, 1997 – 1998
Ramona Palmer, 2001

I want to acknowledge the generous assistance of Ray Randolph, a devoted fan of KHJ, who maintained an extraordinary collection of original material from the station. He provided lists of song titles played on KHJ, and, scans of photographs that date back to the mid-1960s so that my websites could present authentic pictures for you to see.

Last, but not least, thanks to Bill Mouzis (1922 – 2013), who sent me several candid emails throughout the 2000s that helped me understand the historical facts about KHJ during the late 1960s.

Secondary Sources

I also drew from many reports about the radio programming business and Drake-Chenault that appeared either in the print media or on other websites:

Andrews, Dave and Hagerty, Michael, "K100 100.3 'K100 FM,'" http://www.geocities.com/Hollywood/Academy/5515/kiqq.html

"Advisor Becomes Boss: Drake Signs with RKO," *Broadcasting*, 16 October 1972, pp. 61 – 62.

Billboard, January 1965 – January 1976.

Brown, James, "Chenault-Drake Team to Operate K100-FM," *Los Angeles Times*, 5 December 1973, Part IV, p. 34.

_____. "Drake and K100—an Encore in Stereo," *Los Angeles Times Calendar*, 17 March 1974, pp. 74 –75.

Denisoff, R. Serge. *Solid Gold: The Popular Record Industry*. New Brunswick, NJ: Transaction Books, 1975.

Donahue, Tom. "A Rotting Corpse Stinking Up the Airwaves," *Rolling Stone*, 23 November 1967, pp. 14-15.

"Earlybirds of Modern Radio," *Sponsor*, 28 May 1962, pp. 35-59.

"Executioner, The," *Time*, 23 august 1973, p. 48.

Gibson, John. "Bill Drake: Radio's Top 40 Tycoon," *Entertainment World*, 17 April 1970, pp. 8-10.

Los Angeles Times, May 9, 1990, *Calendar* section, page F-1.

"Looking Ahead to Radio in 70's," *Broadcasting*, 13 April 1970, p. 69.

McClay, Bob. "Murray the K on WOR-FM: They Screwed It Up," *Rolling Stone*, 9 November 1967, p. 10.

Passman, Arnold. *The Deejays*. New York: Macmillan, 1971.

"Rock and Roll Muzak," *Newsweek*, 9 March 1970, p. 32.

Selvin, Joel. "Donahue: A True Visionary of Rock." *San Francisco Chronicle*, 3 May 1975, p. 32.

Sculatti, Gene and Van Bebber, Annie. "Drake Back in LA Radio," *Radio & Records*, 7 December 1973, p. 1.

Shearer, Harry. "Captain Pimple Cream's Fiendish Plot," in Eisen, Jonathan, ed. *The Age of Rock: Sounds of the American Cultural Revolution*. New York: Vintage Books, 1969, pp. 357-384.

"Special Report: Radio Programming," *Broadcasting*, 14 December 1964, pp. 57-91.

"Topsy-Turvy World of L.A. Radio," *Rolling Stone*, 28 February 1974, p. 12.

West, Donald. "Special Report: Radio '71." *Broadcasting*, 21 June 1971, pp. 41-80.

For Further Reading

Ron Jacobs wrote *KHJ Inside Boss Radio*, originally published as a paperback book in 2002. I produced the updated eBook version in 2010. Written from his unique perspective, this is for readers who want to understand the day-to-day workings of KHJ, Los Angeles (1965 through 1969) while Jacobs was program director.

Ben Fong-Torres wrote *The Hits Just Keep On Coming: The History of Top 40 Radio*, originally published in November 1998. His book is filled with fascinatingly deep details about KHJ and other top 40 stations you know and love. His book is "as good as it gets" if you're searching for a source with a full and complete account of how top 40 radio in the United States came to be.

About the Author

I maintain an online presence at www.goulartonline.com and you can also visit my professional profile on LinkedIn at www.linkedin.com/in/woodygoulart if you want to learn more about who I am and what I have done along various career paths after rebranding and restarting multiple times.

You can contact me by email at woodygoulart@gmail.com and I will reply.

Woody Goulart
Las Vegas, Nevada

— — — — — — — — — — — —

Made in the USA
Middletown, DE
22 March 2019